An East German border
guard peering through a
crack in the Berlin Wall,
January 1, 1990

Alfred/Sipa

LIFE

100

EVENTS THAT SHOOK OUR WORLD

A HISTORY IN PICTURES OF THE LAST 100 YEARS

The first installment of "Shock and Awe" hitting the western bank of the Tigris River in Baghdad, March 21, 2003

LIFE Books

Editor Robert Andreas
Director of Photography Barbara Baker Burrows
Creative Director Mimi Park
Deputy Picture Editor Christina Lieberman
Writer-Reporters Hildegard Anderson (Chief), Elizabeth Hoover
Copy Wendy Williams (Chief), Christine Q. Brennan, Lesley Gaspar
Production Manager Michael Roseman
Assistant Production Managers Leenda Bonilla, Rachel Hendrick
Photo Assistants Joshua Colow, Eirini Vourloumis
Consulting Picture Editors
Suzanne Hodgart, Mimi Murphy (Rome), Tala Skari (Paris)

Editorial Director Robert Sullivan

President Andrew Blau
Business Manager Roger Adler
Business Development Manager Jeff Burak

Editorial Operations Richard K. Prue (Director),
Richard Shaffer (Manager), Brian Fellows, Raphael Joa,
Stanley E. Moyse (Supervisors), Keith Aurelio, Charlotte Coco,
Erin Collity, Scott Dvorin, Kevin Hart, Rosalie Khan, Marco Lau,
Po Fung Ng, Barry Pribula, Albert Rufino, David Spatz,
Vaune Trachtman, David Weiner

Time Inc. Home Entertainment

Publisher Richard Fraiman
Executive Director, Marketing Services Carol Pittard
Director, Retail & Special Sales Tom Mifsud
Marketing Director, Branded Businesses Swati Rao
Director, New Product Development Peter Harper
Assistant Financial Director Steven Sandonato
Prepress Manager Emily Rabin
Book Production Manager Jonathan Polsky
Marketing Manager Laura Adam
Associate Prepress Manager Anne-Michelle Gallero
Associate Marketing Manager Danielle Radano

Special thanks to Bozena Bannett, Alexandra Bliss,
Glenn Buonocore, Bernadette Corbie, Suzanne Janso,
Robert Marasco, Brooke McGuire, Ilene Schreider, Adriana Tierno

Classic images from the pages and covers of LIFE are now available.
Posters can be ordered at www.LIFEposters.com.
Fine-art prints from the LIFE Picture Collection and the LIFE Gallery
of Photography can be viewed at www.LIFEphotographs.com.

Published by LIFE Books

Time Inc.
1271 Avenue of the Americas, New York, NY 10020

ISBN: 1-932994-10-6
Library of Congress Control Number: 2005902453
"LIFE" is a trademark of Time Inc.

We welcome your comments and suggestions about
LIFE Books. Please write to us at: LIFE Books, Attention:
Book Editors, PO Box 11016, Des Moines, IA 50336-1016

If you would like to order any of our hardcover
Collector's Edition books, please call us at 1-800-327-6388
(Monday through Friday, 7:00 a.m.–8:00 p.m.,
or Saturday, 7:00 a.m.–6:00 p.m., Central Time).

Please visit us, and sample past editions of LIFE, at www.LIFE.com.

Brown Brothers

Introduction

One hundred years is a long time. Not, perhaps, on a tectonic scale, but in ordinary human terms, it is longer than all but a very few of us will live. This volume touches on many of the most important developments that took place during the last 100 years. Sometimes an event's significance was realized only gradually. More often the effect was immediate. It will be noted that recent years are less well represented than earlier ones; a few decades from now that disparity may be corrected. It often takes time to grasp what is truly important. What the 100 have in common is that each reconfigured the fabric of our society in a particular way.

"In a shocking development today . . . " is heard nearly every evening on news broadcasts, although the "shocking development" is often not even the lead item, just another in a half-hour show. Books, newspapers, magazines and the Internet combine for an incessant avalanche of stories about the latest sizzling topics, the vast majority of which will be tepid in a matter of days—and forgotten before the year is out. A quick scan of the pages of this book will reveal people, places and things that will likely continue to resonate for generations to come.

Clearly, the overarching event of our time period

Alice Paul celebrates in 1920 as the 19th Amendment gives women the vote. Paul had fought long and hard for this moment.

An American corpsman gives some candy to a little girl wounded during the D-Day invasion, Normandy, France, June 1944.

was the Second World War. A good case can be made that it was sired at the end of World War I, with the Treaty of Versailles, and given succor with the advent of the Great Depression: In tandem they helped foster an environment suitable for the rise of an Adolf Hitler. World War II itself involved some of history's most spectacular campaigns and indelible personalities, and at its conclusion ushered us into the atomic age. Territorial divisions traced by this conflict helped foment the cold war, which took root almost immediately. There are, accordingly, several entries herein concerning World War II. One that may be less familiar to some American readers involves the Battle of Stalingrad. It was a long, brutal affair, but when it was over, Hitler was prompted to say, "The god of war has gone over to the other side."

Of course, there are plenty of other events to leaven the mix. Radio and television have made the world a global village and provided a variety of programming—for better or worse—to folks in far-flung places. Medical advances have tempered or eliminated suf-

fering that was previously without cure. The arts have enjoyed a fertile epoch, as seen in the tremendous changes marked in each discipline. Consider that popular music before was a matter of folk music and such as Stephen Foster. This is not to say that these forms are lacking, but any time period that includes Louis Armstrong is indeed fortunate. With his style and intelligence, he rearranged the flow of popular music (and made jazz a true art form). Armstrong was a special breed of cat. "We all do 'do, re, mi,'" he said, "but you have to find the other notes yourself."

One hundred years have passed, and our world is quite a different place. Technology hath wrought many changes, but it seems that we are more entwined than ever with fossil fuels. Liberations have abounded: Women are assuming a more equal footing; African Americans are no longer under the boot of the oppressor; and gays, at least in places, have been able to take a stroll down the aisle. To be sure, these groups still face intrinsic social burdens so often inevitable to minorities, but their futures seem different from before. The exploration of outer space is giving us brilliant, real images of what had been the stuff of science fiction. Closer to home, the sexual revolution was launched,

Richard Nixon seems all smiles in August 1974, but he is departing in shame after the Watergate scandal forced him to resign as chief executive.

In January 2005, this child in Sikkal, India, isn't happy she has to get a tetanus shot after the tsunami spread fears of illness across a wide swath.

and, well, it was a sexual revolution.

Is it possible that the next 100 years will generate the same thrills—and the same chills—in equal doses? Is it possible that these coming years will witness change at an even faster pace? Or have these last 100 years been one of a handful of times, like that of ancient Greece or Rome, the Renaissance or the Industrial Revolution, when innovation and drama were the order of the day, when life was truly different from that of other eras? Take a look through the pages of this book, and see what you think.

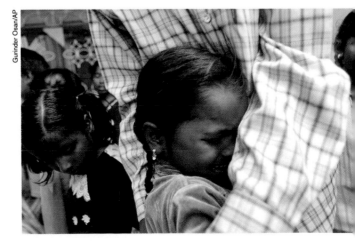
Gurinder Osan/AP

Einstein

1905

Albert Einstein began 1905 as a 25-year-old German émigré living in Bern, Switzerland, and working as a clerk in a patent office. He had never been perceived as a particularly special person, one to keep a close eye on. Then, however, beginning in March, he published papers in four successive months that not only made him one of the world's foremost physicists but also changed the way we regard the universe. These papers dealt with, among other things, the nature of light, and with the size and motion of atoms. The fourth paper—which actually had its genesis in an essay he composed at age 16—revealed Einstein's special theory of relativity and what would come to be called the space-time continuum, in which there is no absolute "frame of reference." Space and time are relative, and the speed of light is the ultimate ruler. Thus, in four months this colossal genius quite simply defined what would become modern physics. And he did not merely rest on his laurels. That September, in an unexpected consequence of his special theory of relativity, Einstein published the most famous equation of all: $E=mc^2$.

Einstein in Paris, 1922

Mechanized Agriculture

Sometimes, what seems to be the most mundane of events turns out to be a moment of serious import. No matter what changes may be afoot in politics, the arts, or science as we know it, there are a handful of constants, and one of these is that human beings must eat to survive. Over the centuries, various advances were made around the world that enhanced the gathering of edibles, but the development of agricultural technology in the 20th century easily outstripped all that came before. There were so many examples of progress that it is difficult to single out just one, but a solid candidate emerged in 1905 when J. Brownlee Davidson of Iowa State College (now University) created the first professional agricultural curriculum. Known as the Father of Agricultural Engineering, Davidson was at the vanguard of innovations in tractors, harvesters, plows and balers that would completely reshape food production—and the nature of food in society. Consider this: At the start of the 20th century, it took four farmers to feed about 10 Americans. By the end of the century, just one farmer could provide for more than 100.

In Mound, Minn., circa 1918, a horse-drawn water truck dwarfed by a steam-powered thresher

1905

The founder of psychoanalysis, Sigmund Freud had in the previous decade established a reputation as a nonconventional thinker, one capable of penetrating insight, when he revealed both his method of using free association to unveil deeper layers in the mind and his explorations into dream interpretation. But when his landmark study *Three Essays on the Theory of Sexuality* appeared in 1905, Freud began to send tremors through the social foundations of the Western world. These societies, with few exceptions, had long kept a tight lid on matters sexual, particularly regarding the sexual development of children. Now such concepts as castration anxiety, oral fixation and penis envy were fodder for genteel conversation, infusing drawing rooms everywhere with a twittery albeit dynamic component. This fellow Freud had stated that sexuality may be the driving force in human behavior. In consequence, many social taboos were reexamined, and there were many religious and educational leaders who were less than delighted. In the coming decades, Freud would have perhaps as many detractors as backers, but his ideas remain compelling a hundred years later.

Freud's Theory of Sexuality

Below, Freud's Vienna study, and the couch used by patients; opposite, strolling in the Bavarian Alps with daughter Anna, herself a distinguished psychoanalyst

Edmund Engelman

Pentecostalism Takes Wing

1906

A one-eyed black preacher named William Joseph Seymour was listening at an open door in 1901 when Kansan Charles Fox Parham declared that speaking in tongues was a sign of baptism in the Holy Ghost. Parham's students and a few others were "speaking" words—not those of any known language but, they claimed, words emanating from divine inspiration. They slowly gathered some adherents, and in 1906 the movement took off when the charismatic Seymour had his own baptism in the Spirit and created a mission in an abandoned church on Azusa Street in Los Angeles. The site attracted black folks and white, rich and poor, Anglos and Latinos. Within two years, missionaries from Seymour's ministry had been dispatched to 25 countries. It has been suggested that a growing indifference to organized religion in the late 19th century set the stage for a new sort of faith, one like Pentecostalism, which eschews such traditional doctrines and theology. Instead, this is an oral religion emphasizing intuitive acts—speaking in tongues, singing, swaying, shouting and dancing. These are avid evangelists compelled to spread the word about the second coming of Christ. And many are listening: It is estimated that of every dozen people in the world today, one is a Pentecostal. It is the fastest-growing Christian movement in the world.

Minister Seymour, seated second from right, in 1909; above, Pentecostal evangelist Aimee Semple McPherson in 1935.

Reginald Fessenden in Chestnut Hill, Mass., on August 29,1924

At nine p.m. on Christmas Eve, 1906, sailors on merchant ships in the Atlantic Ocean were stunned when summoned by their wireless operators for an unexpected holiday miracle, something no one had ever heard before: a radio show. The host was Reginald Aubrey Fessenden, who as a young man had kept a scrapbook full of Edison's achievements, and had even worked for the great man in his New Jersey Laboratory. But on this night, it was Fessenden who was the star, operating out of Brant Rock, Mass., with the aid of 400-foot towers, transcending the mere dots and dashes of the wireless telegraph as he sang and played *O, Holy Night* on his violin. His wife and secretary read a biblical text. "The Father of Radio Broadcasting" also played a recording of Handel's *Largo* before signing off with the words, "Merry Christmas." The 40-year-old Canadian would go on to hold more than 500 patents, but none would have a comparable effect on our world.

1906

First Radio Broadcast

1907 Plastic

Belgian-born inventor Leo Baekeland was looking for a cheap and easily produced substance for electrical insulation in his lab near Yonkers, N.Y. Then he discovered that the gunk that collects after a chemical reaction between phenol (a solvent and disinfectant) and formaldehyde (a gas derived from wood alcohol, used in embalming) made a hard, translucent and infinitely moldable substance. He named his invention Bakelite and marketed it as "the material of a thousand uses." He had created the first entirely synthetic plastic, one that was both inexpensive and versatile, a perfect surrogate for more costly organic materials such as ivory and wood. During the Depression, debutantes found that Bakelite bracelets were a fun (and affordable) substitute for Cartier diamonds. Today, plastic manufacturing is a multibillion-dollar enterprise, and we can't stop finding new uses for the stuff. It's in bullet-resistant vests, heart valves, disposable containers, toys—practically everything we touch daily. It fosters a throwaway culture, and millions upon million of tons of the nonbiodegradable product have collected in landfills, contributing to a global environmental crisis.

A vintage Bakelite radio; bottom, a plastic house at Disneyland in 1958

Photodisc

Bettmann/Corbis

A Ford Model A on the assembly line at the Rouge Plant in Dearborn, Mich., in 1928; Henry Ford, circa 1934

As early as 1811, manufacturers had experimented with rudimentary assembly lines, but it took the genius of a Michigan farm boy to realize their full potential. Henry Ford wanted to build "a motor car for the great multitude," but automobiles were expensive, custom-built machines. He invested five years in studying a variety of industries before finally arriving at the moving assembly line, which allows workers to stand in one place while a conveyor belt brings the product to them. The worker performs his or her one step in the building process, and the product moves on to the next stage. Ford so perfected the assembly line that his Highland Park, Mich., plant could put together a Model T in an hour and a half, and by 1927 a new car rolled off the 250-foot line every 24 seconds. To keep his employees happy—while at the same time fueling sales—the canny Ford paid them an unheard-of five dollars for an eight-hour day (compared with the national average of $2.38 for a nine-hour day) and made car loans available to potential customers. The automobile shortly became a cornerstone of the global economy, and Ford's assembly line a fixture at factories around the world.

1908

Ford's Assembly Line

The Cult of Celebrity Is Born

1910

In the first decade of the 20th century, the fledgling motion pictures business was in the stranglehold of an eastern consortium known as the Trust. Headed by Thomas Edison, these 10 companies controlled production, distribution, pricing—in short, everything. And in order to keep costs as low as possible, they had movie performers toil in anonymity, ensuring that they remain nameless, interchangeable parts. These actors were not faceless, however, and one became known as The Biograph Girl, after the firm whose movies she appeared in. In 1910, a German immigrant named Carl Laemmle forever changed the nature of motion pictures when he lured the actress, whose name was Florence Lawrence, to his company by promising to put her name on the marquee. Then, in a publicity stunt, Laemmle started a rumor that she had been killed by a streetcar, and after garnering attention for this, he took out ads saying that Lawrence was alive and well and would appear in his forthcoming production, *The Broken Oath*. Of course, the Trust had been right all along. Movie stars would soon demand higher and higher salaries—it was, after all, the stars people wanted to see—and today the worship of celebrities continues more vigorously than ever.

Florence Lawrence

Standard Oil Trust Busted

1911

"I believe the power to make money is a gift from God . . . I believe it is my duty to make money and still more money," John D. Rockefeller proclaimed in 1905, and make money he did. He built an empire with his Standard Oil Company, which was so adept at crushing competition it eventually controlled 90 percent of the United States oil market. But President Theodore Roosevelt didn't care much for Rockefeller's "theology" and the government sued Standard Oil on the basis of a little-enforced law, the Sherman Antitrust Act of 1890, which allowed the federal government to intervene if a company grew sufficiently powerful to curtail competition. On May 15 the United States Supreme Court agreed with Roosevelt and ordered the company to dissolve. This landmark decision set the precedent for antitrust actions against such companies as AT&T, Alcoa and Microsoft.

Frank Ehrenford

Below, oilfields near Los Angeles, 1923; right, Rockefeller

Los Angeles Chamber of Commerce

1911

Triangle Shirtwaist Fire

The workday at Triangle Shirtwaist Company in New York City's Greenwich Village was drawing to a close on March 25 when suddenly smoke began to fill the eighth floor and panicked employees realized that a fire had broken out. The workers, mostly women between 13 and 23 years old, desperately made for the exits, but most of the doors were locked to prevent the immigrant laborers from stealing anything. Many couldn't escape because the doors opened inward and the terrified workers were pressed against them. A few managed to crawl out onto the rickety fire escape before it collapsed. Horrified onlookers watched as women jumped to their deaths from the upper floors. In the 18 minutes it took to get the blaze under control, 146 people perished. The resultant public outcry led to a commission on workplace safety as well as the passage of nationwide laws. One member of the commission noted, "Moved by this sense of stricken guilt, we banded ourselves together to find a way by law to prevent this kind of disaster . . . It was the beginning of a new and important drive to bring [humanity] to the lives of the brothers and sisters we all had in the working groups of these United States."

Bettmann/Corbis

Brown Brothers

A city, and a nation, left in shock

Brown Brothers

1912

Titanic

She was the largest, most luxurious ship of her day and, with a double-bottomed hull, thought to be the safest. "Not even God Himself could sink this ship," a crewmember remarked as the liner began her maiden voyage, from Southampton, England, to New York City. But shortly before midnight on April 14, the vessel sideswiped an iceberg near Newfoundland, buckling the hull and puncturing the first six compartments within. She rapidly began to take on water. Passengers rushed to the lifeboats only to find there weren't enough spaces for everyone—even though there were more than required by law. More than fifteen hundred souls were drowned in one of the worst maritime disasters to date. The world was transfixed for months after the tragedy. Newspapers ran updated lists of the dead every day, and readers couldn't get enough stories about the fateful night. As a result of the sinking, the first international convention on safety at sea was held, and strict regulations put into effect. One survivor called the sinking of Titanic "the event which not only made the world rub its eyes and awake, but woke it with a start . . . To my mind the world of today awoke April 15, 1912."

The reading and writing room aboard Titanic; the vessel being groomed in 1911

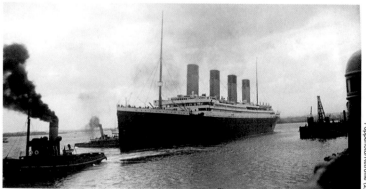

Stravinsky's *The Rite of Spring*

It didn't take very long. The introductory notes of the bassoon—played in a register so high that few would even have known it was a bassoon—set the stage for perhaps the most shocking first night in musical history. So the audience was already stirring when the curtain opened and the modernist movement began in earnest, with a sound so original, so jarring, so eruptive that the crowd began to howl sufficiently enough that the dancers could barely hear their cues. It was May 29, 1913, in Paris, the premiere of Igor Stravinsky's *The Rite of Spring,* a ballet choreographed by Vaslav Nijinsky. The Russian-born Stravinsky had created a score that echoed a new world, one thumping with the sound of dissonant traffic in the streets of a newly mechanized world. The violent rhythms and primitive syncopations nearly fomented a riot in the hitherto sedate Théâtre des Champs-Élysées. It was simply too overwhelming for the audience. And for others, too. When Stravinsky first played the score for Serge Diaghilev, whose ballet company would perform that opening night, the impresario interrupted him at one point to inquire, "Does it go on for long like this?" At least in one sense it did. *The Rite of Spring* is one of history's most influential pieces of music.

A performance of *The Rite of Spring* in 2001 by the Béjart Ballet company in Paris; Stravinsky (left) with Nijinsky in 1911.

World War I

1914

There is no question that storm clouds had been gathering slowly but with increasing darkness over Europe as the 20th century proceeded with its second decade. There seemed at the time a certain inevitability to it all, and it was entirely appropriate that what could have been an event of utter transience turned out to be one of immortality. On June 28, 1914, Austrian Archduke Francis Ferdinand was shot dead in his motorcar in Sarajevo by a Bosnian Serb terrorist named Gavrilo Princip. It might easily have been forgotten; Ferdinand was hardly a beloved figure. Instead, as Barbara Tuchman wrote in *The Guns of August,* "Austria-Hungary, with the bellicose frivolity of senile empires, determined to use the occasion to absorb Serbia." Within days, Germany assured Austria of support should Russia carry out its role of Serbian protector. Troops rapidly gathered along the Russo-Austrian border, followed shortly by overall mobilization. Big things had been set in motion by a little event. Wrote Tuchman: "Appalled upon the brink, the chiefs of state who would be ultimately responsible for their country's fate attempted to back away but the pull of military schedules dragged them forward." When the shooting finally stopped in 1918, the casualties surpassed 37 million, and the legacy of "The War to End All Wars" was to lay the groundwork for World War II.

The Panama Canal Opens

1914

A building endeavor of unprecedented scale began in 1904 after President Theodore Roosevelt secured rights to the Panama Canal Zone. Steam shovels and railroad cars worked around the clock, moving enough dirt to bury the island of Manhattan 12 feet deep. "No single great material work," Roosevelt declared of this effort to link the Pacific and Atlantic oceans, "is as of such consequence to the American people." But despite the enormous advantages in time saved and safer voyages, the attention garnered when the canal officially opened on August 15, 1914, was less than one would have expected. At that moment, most eyes were trained on the looming war in Europe. Nonetheless, the canal made a tremendous difference in the pace of trade. For example, a ship going from New York to San Francisco was spared 7,873 miles of travel around South America. In the year 2000, Panama gained complete control of the Canal, which remains a major shipping route to this day, with nearly 5 percent of total world trade traveling through it each year.

Tourists flocking to the canal's Culebra Cut during excavation

Sovfoto

Culver

The Bolshevik Revolution

1917

When the exiled Vladimir Lenin was smuggled back into Petrograd in October 1917, he prophesied that "an armed uprising is inevitable and that its time has come." In four weeks, the young radical and his Bolshevik brethren overthrew the moderate provisional government in a near-bloodless coup. Lenin led with a promise of "Peace, Land and Bread," pledging to forge a truce with Germany and redistribute property. He reorganized the country into what became known as the Soviet Union, based on Karl Marx's principle of the "dictatorship of the proletariat." Before too long it would become a "dictatorship of repression," a totalitarian police state that filled its gulags and executed millions in political purges; the country's botched economic experiments relegated tens of millions more to poverty. In the second half of the 20th century, the rivalry between the Soviet Union and the United States dominated global politics and fueled a nuclear arms race. It all came to an end in 1989 when the Soviet Union collapsed of its own weaknesses.

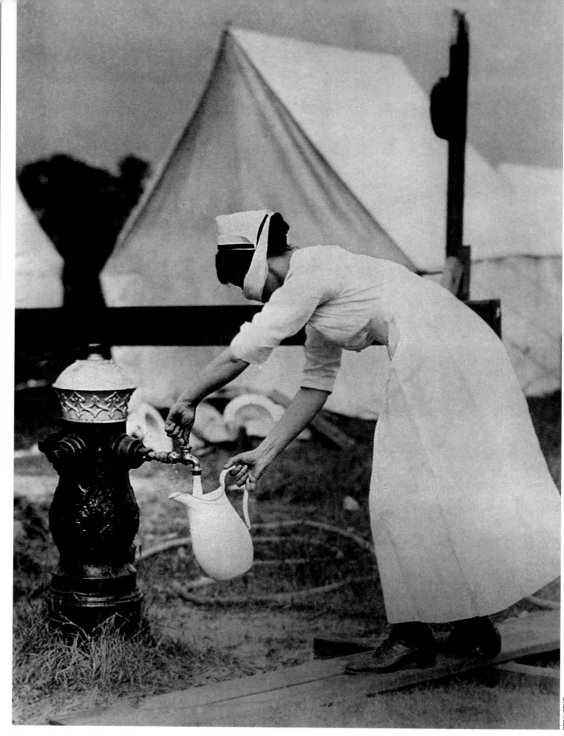

Underwood

A nurse in Brookline, Mass., at a special camp set up for veterans stricken by influenza, September 13, 1918

1918

Influenza Pandemic

In March 1918 a group of soldiers in Kansas contracted a deadly new strain of influenza, known as the Spanish flu. Spread along transportation routes and carried by troops shipped to the front lines of World War I—where the disease killed them as fast as enemy fire—it quickly became a global fiend, extremely potent, capable of killing a human being within hours of the appearance of the first symptom. And nowhere had an acquired immunity to it been established. An army surgeon remembered: "I saw hundreds of young stalwart men in uniform coming into the wards of the hospital. Every bed was full, yet others crowded in . . . In the morning, the dead bodies are stacked about the morgue like cordwood." Although there would be other outbreaks of the flu during the 1920s, the virus mysteriously lost most of its killing power in the spring of 1919. However, by that fated year, an estimated 20 to 40 million people around the world had already lost their lives, making it quite possibly the worst pandemic in history. Half a million Americans had been claimed, 10 times as many as had died in the war.

When the German delegation signed the Treaty of Versailles in the elegant Hall of Mirrors at Louis XIV's former palace outside of Paris, they were denounced at home as traitors and criminals. World War I was finally over, and France and Great Britain, resolute that Germany must never rise again, rejected most of Woodrow Wilson's moderate Fourteen Points proposal in favor of draconian measures against the defeated enemy. The Versailles edict forced Germany to relinquish a tenth of its land and pay reparations beyond what the war-torn country could afford. It also mandated sharp reductions in the army and navy and contained a "war guilt" clause, which blamed the whole affair on Germany. Many Germans felt betrayed, tricked into disarming by Wilson's plan only to have the more lenient terms withdrawn at the signing. In addition to dealing a severe blow to an already ravaged German economy, the agreement made the country a global pariah by excluding it from the League of Nations until 1926. Freeing the homeland from the shackles of Versailles became a rallying cry for Adolf Hitler, who capitalized on festering bitterness and resentment to mobilize support for his fledgling Nazi party.

1919

Treaty of Versailles

Trials

The courtroom, according to man-of-letters H.L. Mencken, is "a place where Jesus Christ and Judas Iscariot would be equals, with the betting odds in favor of Judas." Whatever the odds, nothing takes a firmer grasp of the public's throat than a big trial. The cases here, involving murder, morality and mayhem, were among the most notorious of them all.

1907

Harry K. Thaw enjoys breakfast from the swank Delmonico's restaurant in his New York City cell. In a sweltry love triangle featuring dancer Evelyn Nesbit, the wealthy Thaw killed architect Stanford White and was sent to an asylum. He was later set free.

1925

Clarence Darrow defends John T. Scopes, accused of teaching Darwinism in a Dayton, Tenn., public school. Prosecutor William Jennings Bryan secured a conviction, which was overturned on a technicality.

1935

Carpenter-burglar Bruno Hauptmann was arrested for kidnapping and killing Charles Lindbergh Jr., the son of Anne and "Lucky Lindy." Hauptmann was executed in 1936.

1951

Julius and Ethel Rosenberg
are separated by a screen
in New York City after
their conviction as traitors
who gave the "secret of
the atomic bomb" to
the Soviets. They were
later executed.

1970

Charles Manson is led into jail in L.A. after his arrest in the hideous murder of actress
Sharon Tate and four others. Manson and three female accomplices were sentenced
to death, but that penalty was abolished in California and they are incarcerated for life.

1995

Los Angeles is again
the scene as defense
attorney Johnnie
Cochrane hugs O.J.
Simpson after the ex-
footballer-turned-actor
is acquitted of killing
his wife, Nicole, and
waiter Ronald Goldman.

Prohibition Begins

One of the greatest follies of the 20th century began on January 16, 1920, when the 18th Amendment, banning the making and selling of alcoholic beverages, went into effect. The newly installed Prohibition commissioner proclaimed, "This law will be obeyed in cities large and small, and where it is not obeyed it will be enforced." He couldn't have been more wrong; both local cops and federal agents turned a blind eye (and, perhaps, extended a palm for greasing) as illegal alcohol fueled a nationwide, multimillion-dollar underground industry. The problem was that there were just too many people who wanted alcohol—and deeming it forbidden fruit only served to make it more desirable. American ingenuity showed itself with copper bloomers for smuggling swill under skirts and elaborate alarm systems that warned customers in swank speakeasies of coming raids. By 1926, New York City had more places to tie one on—an estimated 100,000 underground drinking establishments—than when the stuff had been legit. Practically everyone got in on the action, from low-level entrepreneurs with (often dangerous) bathtub gin to the sophisticated (and often deadly) enterprises of gangsters like Al Capone. The rampant flouting of the law prompted President Herbert Hoover to remark on "the futility of the whole business." By February 1933, America had had its fill, so to speak, and the 18th Amendment became the first, and only, amendment ever to be repealed.

At left, a lawman putting the ax to liquor barrels in 1923; opposite, a flapper in 1925, replete with cloche, velvet dress and "concealed" flask

Culver

Culver

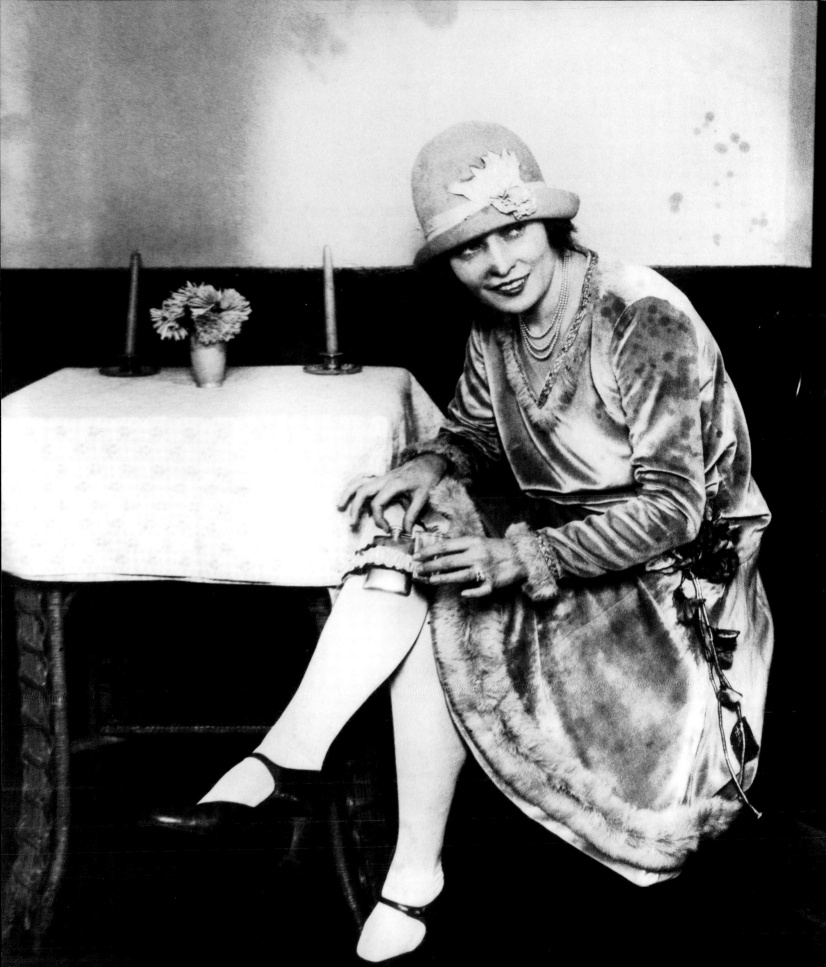

1920

Yankees Acquire Babe Ruth

It's not as though George Herman Ruth wasn't a star when he was with the Boston Red Sox. He was a standout pitcher, might even have been a Hall of Famer just for that. And in his last year with the club, 1919, he led the league in home runs with a record 29. That's why the Yankees purchased him from Boston, casting the longtime spell known as the Curse of the Bambino. In his first year in New York, Ruth stunned the sports world by belting an unheard-of 54 homers, more than any other team! Attendance figures soared, as his "Ruthian" blasts were the stuff of national drama. The Babe was another animal entirely: Everything about him was big. He was much bigger than the average man, and he ate more and drank more and partied more than any other nine guys. "I swing big, with everything I've got. I hit big or miss big. I like to live as big as I can." Off the field, in his trademark camel-hair coat, Ruth was the idol of millions of kids; he visited them in hospitals and signed autographs with that same trademark tirelessness. He is the reason they call Yankee Stadium "The House That Ruth Built." His was a public spectacle unlike anything before, a traveling show that made baseball a spectator sport for all of America, and beyond.

The one and only Babe, 1922

UPI/Bettmann/Corbis

Women Get the Vote

1920

The first time that Congress considered granting women the right to vote was in 1878, at the behest of Susan B. Anthony. Obviously, though, it was not a cut-and-dry issue, as it would remain in debate for the next 41 years. Along the way, the fervor of a group of suffragettes spread nationwide, and women took to the streets en masse, including the 8,000 who descended on Woodrow Wilson's inauguration. At long last, their demand was met on August 26, 1920, when, in front of a group of all-male invitees, the 19th Amendment was certified. Twenty-six million adults were newly enfranchised—just in time for the fall election. The founder of the League of Women Voters commented, "Winning the vote is only an opening wedge . . . but to learn to use it is a bigger task." Since that day, women have clearly learned how to use the vote; by the year 2000, women were more likely to vote than men. Some pundits even suggested that women, traditionally Democratic but concerned about national security matters, swung the election by voting for George W. Bush in 2004.

Suffragettes preparing for a parade in 1912

"April is the cruellest month, breeding/Lilacs out of the dead land, mixing/Memory and desire, stirring/Dull roots with spring rain." With these memorable lines begins one of the most famous of all poems, *The Waste Land,* written by T.S. Eliot, who was born in St. Louis but settled in England as a young man. The postwar sensation of futility encumbered by an increasingly fragmented culture is spectacularly limned in Eliot's work, which marks a clean break with the poetic past. To come to grips with the complexities of the modern world, Eliot had to communicate in a new, different manner. To accomplish this he leaned heavily on the economy of allusion, often from ancient cultures, to the extent that he chose to include profuse footnotes. These daunting classical references were simply too much for many, who ridiculed the demands of the poem. Ironically, however, Eliot was also a fervent advocate of ordinary language, which is arranged throughout *The Waste Land* in a brilliant tango with the high-toned language it connects with. Indeed, the poem is a constantly shifting extravaganza of forms and tones and textures, suggesting the dislocation of modernity in an execution theretofore unimagined. Eliot's stark, ironic assessment of the 20th century would inform countless artists to come.

Eliot in London, 1958

Larry Burrows

1925

Louis Armstrong's Hot Five

He was born in New Orleans in 1901, and had a rough-and-tumble upbringing that included his shooting off a pistol in the street to celebrate New Year's Eve when he was 11. That landed Louis Daniel Armstrong a year in the Colored Waifs' Home, where—Huzzah!—he learned to play various instruments in the brass band. He soon came under the wing of cornetist King Oliver, who summoned Armstrong to play for his Chicago band in 1922. Satchmo simply wowed people with his inventiveness, range and a pure, ethereal tone that will never be equaled. Three years later he signed to record with the OKeh label in Chitown. Nobody was ready for the revolutionary music that Armstrong and his handpicked Hot Five (and later Hot Seven) would produce. The combos drew from an expansive repertory, and there had never been a star leader like Armstrong, one who played, sang, joked and dominated with his irresistible personality. Audiences who hadn't given jazz a second thought devoured this new, succulent sound, and when they heard the man scat, well that was that. As trumpeter Hugh Masekela said, "Before Louis Armstrong, the world was definitely square, just like Christopher Columbus thought."

Louis Armstrong and his golden trumpet

1927

Lucky Lindy

At 7:54 a.m. on May 20, 1927, a 25-year-old airmail pilot took off from Roosevelt Field on Long Island, N.Y., barely clearing the telephone wires at the end of the runway. When he touched down in Paris the next day, Charles Lindbergh was engulfed by a delirious crowd of nearly 100,000. He had completed the first nonstop solo transatlantic flight in his custom-built *Spirit of St. Louis.* According to *National Geographic,* "He took off as an unknown boy from rural Minnesota and landed 33 and a half hours later . . . as the most famous man on Earth and sent the world into an unprecedented frenzy." When he returned to the States, Lindbergh was greeted by four million fans in a New York City ticker-tape parade and given the Congressional Medal of Honor. Lindbergh then crisscrossed the United States, tirelessly promoting aviation, which he had shown could be safe and reliable. National obsession with Lindbergh peaked in 1932 with the kidnapping and murder of his son, and the family moved to Europe in search of privacy. In the coming years, he would be viewed as a misguided isolationist, a Nazi sympathizer even, but for the great majority of Americans he would remain one of the country's foremost heroes.

On the victory tour, June 6, 1927, the Croydon Aerodrome in London

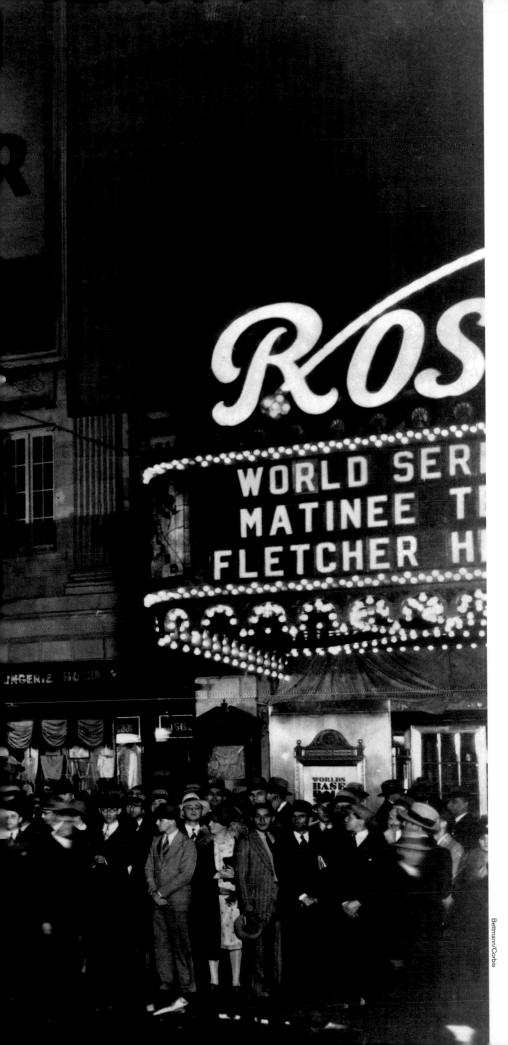

The Jazz Singer

1927

"In every living soul, a spirit cries for expression." So reads the opening title card to perhaps the most important motion picture ever made, *The Jazz Singer*. And the words were entirely apt, as they marked the occasion of an art form come to full bloom—or at least the occasion which made such a thing possible, for this was the first time that a feature-length film used synchronized speech as well as music and sound effects. The star was Al Jolson, a high-voltage Russian-born entertainer who was a big success in vaudeville and on Broadway. Audiences were beside themselves when they suddenly heard Jolie *talking,* and his first words were just right: "Wait a minute! Wait a minute! You ain't heard nothin' yet!" He was actually talking to technicians and others on the set, but the filmmakers cleverly left this in, along with other improvised remarks. The movie's plot was trite, but that didn't matter. People were thrilled to hear sound, which meant the silents were done for, as was vaudeville itself—a huge national business that instantly seemed prehistoric. The talkie made Warner Bros. a major studio, and also linked motion pictures to a variety of other industries.

A crowd in New York City waiting to hear what they ain't heard yet

INCUBATOR
NO
ADMITTANCE

Fritz Goro

Penicillin

When Scottish physician Alexander Fleming went on vacation in 1928, he left a dish smeared with Staphylococcus bacteria on a bench in his laboratory. In his absence, a mold from another lab drifted onto the culture. When Fleming returned, he noticed that the bacteria had not grown where the mold had fallen. Fleming (who would later be knighted) named the active ingredient in the mold penicillin but was unable to purify it into a usable medicine. In 1939 a research team at Oxford University headed by Australian Howard Florey (also later knighted) refined Fleming's specimen, and produced the first safe and effective antibiotic. During World War II, with soldiers dying from infected wounds on the front lines, Florey's team helped galvanize the large-scale production of penicillin, enough to save millions of lives. The remarkable antibiotic also proved effective against pneumonia and diphtheria—previously considered incurable—and made surgery and childbirth safer by reducing the body's vulnerability to infection. Today penicillin remains one of the most common and effective antibiotics in the world.

Mold cultures for the mass production of penicillin at Squibb Laboratories in New Brunswick, N.J., in 1943

The Stock Market Crash

1929

During the 1920s, many Americans invested in the stock market because they were able to use credit instead of cash to purchase shares. With so many people buying, stock prices soared. On October 24, 1929, "Black Thursday," investors, fearing the bubble would burst, frantically sold off their holdings, and prices plummeted. Banks that had provided the initial credit were now unable to collect from their destitute debtors, and, what was worse, they had invested depositors' money in the now-worthless stocks. People literally rushed to banks only to find them empty, and yet the disaster had just begun. Without any investment capital, businesses failed, leaving crops to rot in the fields and factory doors slammed by foreclosure. The Great Depression quickly took its toll, and by 1933 about a quarter of the American workforce was unemployed. Inflation and unemployment were not just American problems, either, as their effects resounded across the globe.

Oakland Museum/Dorothea Lange Co.

An unlucky speculator and his roadster in New York in 1929; at right, in San Francisco in '33, an all-too-familiar breadline

The Granger Collection

$100 WILL BUY THIS CAR MUST HAVE CASH LOST ALL ON THE STOCK MARKET

Trying to cope with
the floodwaters,
Hankou, 1931

Yangtze River Flood

1931

At 3,915 miles, the Yangtze River is the third longest in the world and China's principal inland waterway, linking vital seaports with major cities in a vast and important transportation network. Unfortunately, the monsoon rains frequently create havoc with the river and its many tributaries, leading to heavy flooding. If the main artery overflows at the same time as the tributaries, the result is often wicked. At least 10 times in the past century, areas along the Yangtze have been inundated, but the worst was surely the nightmare of 1931. There had been a severe drought during the three previous years, then heavy rain fell without pause in May and June, creating six giant flood waves that obliterated dams and levees in two dozen places, leaving water over 35,000 square miles of land. Population centers like Nanking and Wu-han were hit hard; Wu-han had water—more than 20 feet high in places—for four months. In the end, disease, starvation and drowning claimed 3.7 million lives, and fully one quarter of China's population was affected by the calamity.

The Empire State Building

It was the depths of the Depression, but General Motors simply could not go on with rival Chrysler owning the New York City skyline, so GM plunged $40 million into a building endeavor that would thrill for the ages. When the Empire State Building opened on May 1, 1931, the nation cheered this bravura edifice. Completed in a mind-boggling 410 days, the 1,454-foot-high building enjoyed a 40-year reign as the world's tallest. Having since been surpassed in height, it resolutely remains the most beloved skyscraper on the planet, the stuff of legend: In 1933, that regal émigré from a faraway island, King Kong, toppled from its elegant art deco façade, and, in 1957's *An Affair to Remember,* Cary Grant anxiously awaited Deborah Kerr on the observation deck (a sightseeing perch that still accommodates 3.5 million visitors a year). The actress Fay Wray, who was dragged to the Empire State Building's apex by the giant ape, captured the feelings of many who have looked aloft at this revered icon: "I . . . feel as though it belongs to me or is it vice versa?"

Former governor Al Smith at the building's opening

Orations

"Churchill wrote his own speeches. When a leader does that, he becomes emotionally invested with his utterances . . . If Churchill had had a speech writer in 1940, Britain would be speaking German today," said author James C. Humes. Winston Churchill was certainly one of the foremost orators of the last 100 years, but each of these other men had a way with a word as well.

1938

President Franklin D. Roosevelt delivered many talks (here, on November 4) over the radio. They were often "fireside chats" that bolstered the nation during the Depression and World War II.

1939

His nickname as a ballplayer said it all: The Iron Horse. But even Lou Gehrig couldn't fend off the disease that would take his name. On July 4, he spoke in Yankee Stadium: "Fans, for the past two weeks you have been reading about the bad break I got. Yet today I consider myself the luckiest man on the face of the earth."

1950

During his decades as a leader of the British Empire, Churchill (here, in Leeds) provided countless brilliant, stirring orations.

1952

Richard Nixon was running for Vice President when he was accused of fiscal malfeasance. On September 23 he cleared the air with a televised itemization of his finances, and references to such as wife Pat's "respectable Republican cloth coat." There had been one political gift: a cocker spaniel named Checkers. "And you know, the kids, like all kids, love the dog, and . . . regardless of what they say about it, we're gonna keep it."

1963

Few moments have been more important to a race–the human race–than when Rev. Martin Luther King Jr. delivered his I Have a Dream speech on August 28 from the steps of the Lincoln Memorial in Washington, D.C.

1987

The cold war was clearly thawing when President Ronald Reagan stood before Berlin's historic Brandenburg Gate. Flush with the impending Free World victory, he called forth to his Soviet counterpart, "Mr. Gorbachev, tear down this wall!"

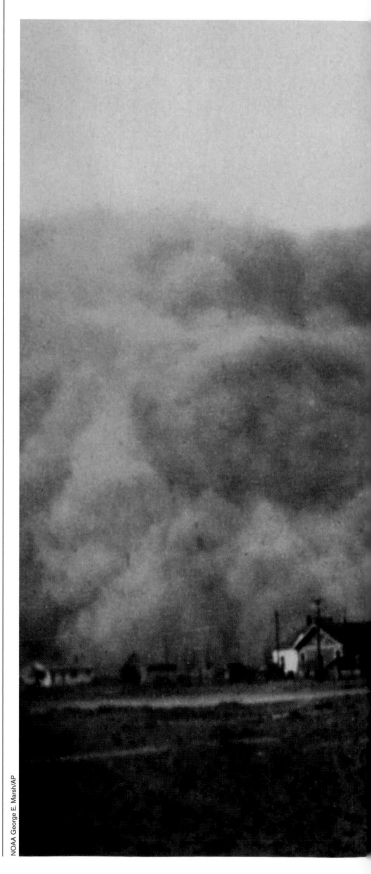

A dust storm engulfing Stratford, Tex., on April 18, 1935; above, Dorothea Lange's photo of migrants from Deadwood, S.D., taken in Tule Lake, Calif.

This wasn't something that happened overnight. The roots, so to speak, were planted during World War I when high wheat prices and hungry troops led farmers in the prairie states to plow and seed lands that had been used for grazing cattle. Little consideration was given to proper soil management, and the terrain was drastically overcultivated. Things were O.K. during the '20s, and then 1931 yielded a bumper crop. Wheat prices plummeted, and some farms were left deserted. A prolonged drought set in, and a horrible process began. As if a Great Depression in high gear wasn't enough, the fields turned bone dry, and the winds kicked up, and some 300,000 square miles of earth that had once been protected by buffalo grass was open to ruin. The soil couldn't hold the spring crops. Moreover, these weren't ordinary winds but "black blizzards" that left people and animals lost and in harm's way, helpless before storms like the one in 1935 that wrecked half the wheat crop in Kansas, a quarter of it in Oklahoma and all of it in Nebraska. The dust was sometimes blown as far east as the Atlantic, while a lot of the people were carried west in search of jobs. Their painful plight was achingly documented in works by Dorothea Lange, Woody Guthrie and John Steinbeck.

NOAA George E. Marsh/AP

1932

First Blood Bank

In the early 19th century physicians began experimenting with blood transfusions, but without methods to prevent clotting, their efforts were crude at best. A century later, in World War I France, preservation techniques pioneered at New York City's Mount Sinai Hospital enabled Dr. Oswald Hope Robertson to carry blood to the front lines in makeshift ice chests. Despite his success, the first civilian blood bank didn't open until 1932, in Leningrad, when the Soviet Union began to develop a nationwide system for collecting, storing and distributing blood. Five years later, Dr. Bernard Fantus opened the first U.S. blood bank, at Cook County Hospital in Chicago, and others quickly followed. It is difficult to overestimate their importance. As American Red Cross President and CEO Marty Evans said in 2003, "To a child battling sickle cell anemia, a grandmother fighting leukemia or a father waiting for a liver transplant, having a safe and available blood supply is more than a wish—it's a necessity."

A blood supply depot in England during World War II

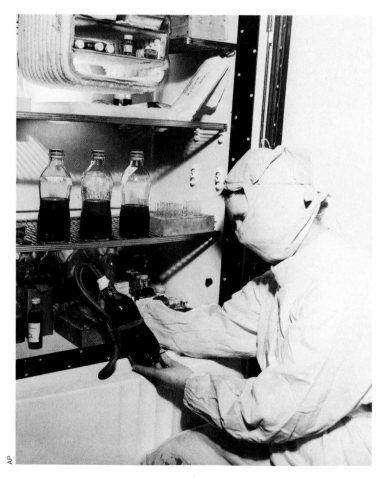

1933

The New Deal

Franklin D. Roosevelt, waving from car, at a Civilian Conservation Corps camp in Virginia's Shenandoah Valley, August 12, 1933

In 1932, the American electorate desperately wanted a leader who would take active steps to yank them out of their economic morass. They opted for Franklin Roosevelt, who immediately rolled up his sleeves to provide relief in the form of unemployment compensation and agricultural subsidies. FDR also created a cavalcade of programs, such as the Public Works Administration and the Civilian Conservation Corps, providing thousands of jobs building bridges, highways and dams. Further, Roosevelt ushered in a new era of bank regulations with the creation of the Federal Deposit Insurance Corporation, which insures bank deposits, and the Securities and Exchange Commission, which safeguards would-be investors from unscrupulous hucksters. Roosevelt's New Deal changed the function of the federal government with respect to the economy; Washington was henceforth expected to step in and do something when the going got rough, which included providing some safety nets for citizens. Finally, the New Deal protected workers in their later years, as well, with the Social Security Act of 1935, mandating a national pension system.

Hitler Comes to Power

World War I had been a catastrophe for Germany, a drawn-out debacle that ended in stunning defeat, exacerbated by the war-guilt clause and staggering financial reparations meted out at Versailles. Some Germans were stoic, but others felt wronged, and agonized over the sorry lot of a once-proud nation beset by poverty. In such an environment, compounded by inept Weimar leadership, an Austrian-born veteran of the war conspired in 1923 with a famous general to overthrow the government. This Beer Hall Putsch failed and left Adolf Hitler briefly behind bars, giving the zealot the opportunity to dictate a book called *Mein Kampf,* which laid out his distrust of democracy, his fear of Communism and his loathing of Jews. Most Germans paid him little attention, at least at first, but his firebrand orations and incisive grasp of human frailties increasingly won him adherents who basked in his vision of a strong Germany ruled by the Aryan people. Hitler lost out in a presidential election in 1932, but the next year was appointed chancellor. When the president died in 1934, Hitler fused both titles into one: Führer. His inhumanly brutal tactics killed off any opposition, and the world watched passively as one grotesque incident followed another, until war once more seemed quite natural.

Hitler arriving at a youth rally in Berlin

Bettmann/Corbis

Long and Owens during the long-jump competition, August 8, 1936

1936

Jesse Owens Triumphs at the Olympics

When Hitler took control of Germany in 1933, he was delighted that the International Olympic Committee had, five years earlier, awarded the 1936 Games to Berlin. They would provide a tremendous opportunity to demonstrate to the world the supremacy of the Aryan athlete. In one sense, the Olympics were a success for the Nazis, as the host team won far more medals than any other nation. However, the undisputed hero of the Games turned out to be James "Jesse" Cleveland Owens, the son of an African American sharecropper. Owens won four gold medals, and despite fears that he would be heckled, he became a huge crowd favorite. He also got along swimmingly with Hitler's fair-haired track star, Luz Long. In fact, when Owens got into foul trouble in the long jump, the German gave him a tip that helped Owens beat Long in the event. Back in the States, ticker-tape parades awaited Owens, along with an understanding of his place in society: "Until the '30s, the Negro had no image to point to. Then there were two—Joe Louis and myself."

Germany Invades Poland

The concept of *Lebensraum* ("living space") had long been central to Adolf Hitler's geopolitical vision. In 1938, Nazi Germany annexed Austria and occupied Czechoslovakia. But Hitler wanted still more land, and he looked eastward. Diplomatic efforts on several fronts to avoid cataclysm were futile, and at 4:45 a.m. on September 1, 1939, German forces unleashed a savage blitzkrieg on Poland. Two days later, Britain and France, honoring commitments to the besieged nation, declared war on Germany. World War II had begun. Poland fought bravely, but horses and swords were no match for tanks. Germany's Luftwaffe destroyed most of the Polish air force before it ever left the ground. All too soon, the capital city came under the gun. As Winston Churchill wrote, "The resistance of Warsaw, largely arising from the surge of its citizens, was magnificent and forlorn. After many days of violent bombardment . . . the Warsaw radio ceased to play the Polish National Anthem, and Hitler entered the ruins of the city."

German troops parading through Warsaw, October 1, 1939, exactly one month to the day after World War II began

A direct hit on the forward magazines of the destroyer *Shaw*

Pearl Harbor
1941

War was raging in Europe, and Germany appeared unstoppable. But the U.S., for better or worse, had stayed out of the fray. In Asia, Japan had invaded China in 1937 and had formed an alliance in 1940 with the Axis powers. Relations between Japan and America had withered in the previous decade to the extent that, by late 1941, virtually all commercial and financial ties had been severed. In retrospect, war between the two nations was inevitable . . . in retrospect. At 7:55 a.m. on December 7, things were status quo at the Pearl Harbor naval base in Hawaii. The entire U.S. Pacific fleet, with the exception of its three aircraft carriers, was there. It was a lazy, lovely Sunday morning. The attack was sudden and without warning. Most of the damage was done within a half hour. When it was over, 3,581 Americans were dead or wounded, and 18 ships sunk or seriously damaged. Radio reports of the surprise strike hit the mainland like a knife in the back. Somehow, America had been caught napping. The country would survive, and, as the mastermind of the attack, Adm. Isoroku Yamamoto, had feared, the sleeping giant was awakened—and filled with a terrible resolve.

1942

Rosie the Riveter

Margaret Bourke-White

Brown Brothers

Welders in a Gary, Ind., steel mill, January 1942

In the five months following Pearl Harbor, 750,000 women reported for duty at armament plants across the nation, eager to step in and lend a hand with the war effort. Huge numbers of men were joining the service, so stay-at-home moms packed their lunch pails, and those who had previously toiled as underpaid secretaries and domestics landed good jobs for decent money. The nation was captivated by images of "Rosie the Riveter," who proudly flexed her biceps for government propaganda posters. (Rosie may have been based on a real-life worker of the same name who, with another woman, pounded a record 3,345 rivets into a fighter plane in six hours.) By war's end, more than six million women had entered the labor force, and their visible presence on assembly lines challenged prewar assumptions about their roles. Those who worked were profoundly affected by their experiences. As one reflected, "Women did change. They had gotten the feeling of their own money. Making it themselves." Despite the fact that with the advent of peace many were squeezed out of their jobs or elected to return to the home, women remained in the workforce in greater numbers than before—numbers that continue to grow.

Battle of Stalingrad

In mid-1942 the overall feeling in Nazi Germany was one of confidence. Matters were well in hand in Western Europe. On the eastern front, although a bid to take Moscow in the previous December had been thwarted at the last moment by weather and a lack of supplies, there had been many victories to savor. Hitler now had his eyes firmly set on Stalingrad, the third-largest Soviet city and a vital link to the Caspian Sea via the Volga River. What's more, Hitler yearned to seize the city that bore the name of an ardent foe. The assault began that summer, and the fighting was ferocious from the outset. Despite the desperate Soviet defense—Stalin had called for the execution of any who retreated—the Germans advanced until they held almost the entire city. Then in November the Soviets launched a pincer attack and encircled the Germans, removing any possibility of supplies getting through. The winter was frigid, and the Nazis were in their summer uniforms. Ammunition was running out, and they were forced to eat the bones of horses. At last, on January 31, despite Hitler's edict to the contrary, they surrendered. Germany had lost a quarter million men, huge amounts of matériel and all of their momentum. In what has been called the largest battle in history, the Soviet casualties were unimaginable.

Red Army soldiers fighting amid
the rubble that is Stalingrad.

1944

D-Day

The largest invasion in history was supposed to take place in May 1944, but the elements would not permit it, so it was reslated for June 5. But on that day the English Channel had its worst weather in a quarter century. Finally, despite uncertain forecasts but with an assault force haggard from false starts, Gen. Dwight D. Eisenhower, the head of Allied operations in Europe, gave the go-ahead for June 6. Operation Overlord commenced before dawn, as an armada of 7,000 ships and landing craft and 10,000 planes carried some 156,000 Allied troops to the shores of Normandy, in northern France. The German defense, under Field Marshal Erwin Rommel, was intense, but not what the Nazis had promised. Once more, military blunders by Adolf Hitler dimmed German hopes for a large counterattack. Losses on both sides were heavy, and personal heroics many. The sheer size of the invasion, and the fact that its success signaled a death knell for Nazi Germany, has prompted countless retellings. Indeed, the very magnitude of D-Day provides one of the marvels of the 20th century: How, with all those men and machines swarming over southern England, were the Allies able to keep the landing site a secret from Germany?

The first wave of landing craft

John Florea

Brown Brothers

Nordhausen concentration camp, April 1945

As 1945 opened, it was clear that the Allies would emerge victorious in Europe. The fury of battle had not lessened, but the circle of pressure on the Germans grew tighter with each day. Customarily, there would have been a sensation of, if not joy, at least a job well done as the end drew near. But something happened that clouded any hope for unbridled celebration. It began in late January as the Soviets advanced through Poland. Although they were all too well accustomed to the horrors of war, they were hardly prepared for Auschwitz, a hellhole containing several thousand starving, brutalized prisoners, mostly Jews. These were human beings whom the Nazis regarded as inferior, so they were tattooed with numbers and turned into a slave labor operation subject to the vilest sort of medical experimentation and tortures beyond compare. Soon other concentration camps would be discovered: On April 4, American army units came upon the village of Ohrdruf, the site of a deserted camp that had held some 10,000 men. Few had survived. On April 12, Eisenhower and Gen. Omar Bradley inspected Ohrdruf. Said Bradley, "The smell of death overwhelmed us." Eisenhower was enraged and ordered that any such camp was to be documented with film and photographs. Three days later, the British liberated Bergen-Belsen, "home" to 60,000 prisoners. Pictures of thousands of gaunt corpses being bulldozed into a mass grave reached the world, and the unthinkable became inescapable.

1945

The Concentration Camps

Hiroshima

The war in Europe was over, but in the Pacific, despite almost certain defeat, Japanese defenders were making the ultimate sacrifice rather than give up. If Japan refused to surrender, the requisite island-by-island combat promised to be harrowing. None of that would come to pass, however. On August 6, 1945, Col. Paul Tibbets and the crew of the *Enola Gay* (named after the pilot's mother) took off from a little isle called Tinian and headed for the Japanese city of Hiroshima. Aboard the B-29 was a 9,000-pound atomic bomb, the result of years of secret work by the Manhattan Project in the deserts of New Mexico. Hiroshima had been chosen because it was an industrial seaport with a military base, and as it had not yet been bombed, it would provide untainted evidence of the new weapon's power. At 8:15 a.m. the bomb exploded 1,900 feet above the city. The tail gunner described the mushroom cloud as "a spectacular sight, a bubbling mass of purple-gray smoke and you could see it had a red core in it and everything was burning inside." An estimated 80,000 died. Three days later, a bigger bomb fell on Nagasaki, instantly killing 40,000. The nature of this atomic destruction, the enormity of it, was, of course, without precedent; Japan surrendered on August 14. The shadow of the mushroom cloud is with us still, as is the debate over whether such annihilation was necessary.

Hiroshima, October 1, 1945, two months after the blast

U.N. Charter Signed

1945

The League of Nations was formed in the wake of World War I to prevent a repetition of such massive bloodshed. Clearly, it had been unable to do the job. With World War II in full swing, the Allies convened in 1944 for nine weeks in Washington, D.C., to lay the groundwork for a stronger international organization. Their proposal was refined in the following year when delegates from 50 countries met in San Francisco to prepare the United Nations charter. In a solemn ceremony at the War Memorial Opera House, a representative from each country signed the document, pledging "to save succeeding generations from the scourge of war . . . to reaffirm faith in fundamental human rights . . . to establish conditions under which justice and respect for . . . international law can be maintained." On October 24, 1945, the requisite number of countries ratified the charter. In the ensuing years, the U.N. has proved a major force, dispatching blue-helmeted peacekeeping troops to quell strife and dispense humanitarian aid. And yet, its efforts have been criticized for going too far, and for not going far enough. But whenever cries ring out that something better is needed, all proposals inevitably lead back to a similar model.

The chairman of the Chinese delegation signing the charter

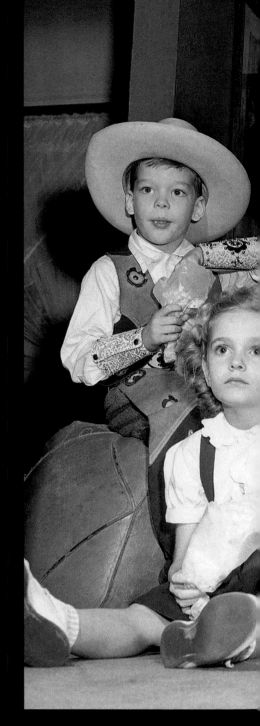

1946

The Baby Boom

Underwood

Hypnotized by *Hopalong Cassidy,* Chicago, 1950

Soldiers had been away from home for a while, in some cases a long while, so as they began to return from World War II, couples were eager to start families, and the birthrate rose around the world. But the baby boom really exploded in the United States, where maternity wards were swamped, elementary schools packed and baby-food aisles empty. Owing to their sheer numbers, the nearly 77 million Americans who entered the world between 1946 and 1964 became a cultural force to be reckoned with. Boomers shaped the political landscape, witnessing—or participating in—the civil rights movement, women's lib, the Summer of Love, Woodstock and the Vietnam War. "If you think you're tired of hearing about us, you should try being one of us," quipped American writer Anna Quindlen. We are not likely to stop hearing about them anytime soon, as the last of the boomers are rounding 40 and, in conjunction with medical advances, creating concerns about the impact of an unprecedentedly large retired population.

Levittown, Long Island, N.Y.

Levittown

1947

By the mid-1940s, an acute housing crunch was forcing recently returned GIs and their new families to bunk in unused army barracks or cram into crowded apartments. A Brooklyn builder named William Levitt tackled the problem by using assembly-line techniques to construct houses quickly and cheaply. He chose former potato farms 25 miles east of Manhattan to develop what he called Levittown. The site consisted of thousands of nearly identical residences. Each had an "expansion" attic, two bedrooms, a kitchen, a bathroom and a living room (which, by 1950, came with a built-in TV set). People camped out overnight for a chance to buy one. Levittown was a rousing success, although in time the community would come to symbolize mass conformity as the residents lived under the watchful eye of Levitt, who regulated how they maintained their lawn and hung their laundry. And, shamefully, for years owners' contracts forbade resale to African Americans. In any case, Levitt's plan left other builders scrambling to keep up, often adopting his methods and luring buyers farther from the city. The growing suburbs would remold the nation's landscape; of the 13 million homes built in the 1950s, only two million were within city limits.

1947

The Marshall Plan

Children in Coventry savoring sandwiches and soup; at top, a large grain warehouse in Marseille

Battered by a long war and one of the worst winters on record, the European economy was in shambles. In this unstable atmosphere, Communist parties flexed their muscles in Italy and France, and the Soviet Union seemed hungry for expansion. In a June 5 commencement speech at Harvard, Secretary of State George C. Marshall—who had been chief of staff of the U.S. Army during WW II—outlined a bold plan to prevent Europe from tumbling deeper into chaos. Marshall proposed that the U.S. provide substantial aid to nations who agreed to buttress one another's shaky economies. A year later, a successful Soviet-backed coup in Czechoslovakia helped persuade Congress to approve $13.1 billion for the Marshall Plan. Shiploads of goods arrived in Europe, carefully labeled so there would be no mistaking the source of the manna. By 1952, when the program had officially ended, Western European industrial output was one third better than it had been before the war. "Ordinary thanks are inadequate . . . Here is one of the most brilliant successes in the history of international relations," gushed one British newspaper.

Ebbets Field, Brooklyn, 1947

Jackie Robinson Breaks the Color Barrier

1947

"If they can fight and die on Okinawa, Guadalcanal [and] in the South Pacific, they can play ball in America." So said the new baseball commissioner, Happy Chandler, in 1945. There had been many African American stars, like Buck Leonard and Rube Foster, but they were shamefully confined to the Negro Leagues. After the war, the time finally seemed right for a change—at least to some—but who would that player be? Two more years would pass before Brooklyn Dodgers President Branch Rickey selected a man with the potent combination of intelligence, maturity and athletic skill. Jackie Robinson was born in Georgia in 1919 and was raised by his mother, a domestic. He became a four-sport star at UCLA, and in WW II, he rose to the rank of second lieutenant. Rickey chose Robinson because he was tough enough not to fight back against the endless slurs and name-calling he would endure. Jackie Robinson was tough enough to turn the other cheek, which he did from his first game, on April 15, 1947, until the 1949 season, when he was turned loose and his intense fires were at last completely on display. That year he was the National League MVP, and there would be many other honors. What he meant to American blacks cannot be overestimated. He gave them pride and the conviction not to back down anymore.

Chuck Yeager always said there's no such thing as a natural-born pilot, but this fella was about as close as they come. Born in rural West Virginia in 1923, he enlisted in the Army when he was just out of high school, and flew 64 missions in Europe during World War II. He shot down 13 Nazi planes, including five in one day. After the war, U.S. aeronautical experiments concentrated on the effects of sonic speeds on planes, and Yeager proved a brave and durable test pilot. He and his cronies had a certain swagger they tossed about nonchalantly at Muroc Army Air Base in California's Mojave Desert. On October 12, 1947, Yeager busted a couple of ribs when a horse threw him, but that didn't stop him two days later when at 5,000 feet he climbed from a B-29 into a suspended X-1 rocket plane called *Glamorous Glennis* (after his wife), rose above 40,000 feet and at last did what most people, even many scientists, thought impossible: He broke the sound barrier, surpassing Mach 1, or about 662 miles per hour. Down on the desert floor they heard a thrilling new sound—the sonic boom. Incidentally, as Tom Wolfe pointed out in *The Right Stuff,* it is Yeager's hillbilly twang that has informed the easygoing voices of airline pilots for decades.

Archetypal test pilot Yeager

1947

huck Yeager Break the Sound Barrier

Mr. Television

Attempts at a working television system began as long ago as the late 19th century, and advances with the medium continued to be made during the subsequent decades. Yet even after World War II the television remained an exotic device, having little to do with the lives of most people. That all changed in September 1948 when a radio and vaudeville veteran with a quick wit and few inhibitions became the host of a variety show originally called *Texaco Star Theater.* Every Tuesday at eight p.m., things got going with a musical intro that featured the irrepressible Milton Berle in an outlandish costume, frequently an absurd dress. There were sundry performers—singers, acrobats, ventriloquists—but "Uncle Miltie" became the focus of the hour, as he spewed out old jokes somehow made irresistibly funny with sight gags and props. The show, an instant success, made Berle television's first superstar. Suddenly people had to be home to see his show, and he became known as Mr. Tuesday Night. The TV set was no longer just a toy, but a fixture in people's lives. Although Berle's star eventually faded, television would become increasingly important, one of the most dynamic inventions of all time.

Terpsichoreans Milton Berle and Ethel Merman

Above, a girl and her father on May 14, 1948; at right, also in '48, young women working the fields in the Galilee region of Israel, ready to fight at a moment's notice

Israel 1948

In the late 1800s, Zionists began pressing for a Jewish homeland in Palestine, despite the presence of fierce Arab opposition. During the ensuing decades, tension came to a boil as Jews escaping Nazi Germany flooded the area (which was then under British mandate). Having made irreconcilable promises to both Arabs and Jews, England looked to the United Nations for a workable solution. In November 1947, the General Assembly adopted, over strenuous Arab objections, a plan to divide the tract into two nations: one Arab and one Jewish. On May 14, 1948, the State of Israel was formally proclaimed; however, peace would last for less than two days before Israel was invaded by Arabs complaining they were forcibly displaced. By the time a shaky armistice was reached eight months later, Israel had gathered more land, while thousands of displaced Palestinians huddled in camps along the West Bank. These soon became tinderboxes of resentment and frustration, as the refugees continually demanded the "right of return." Since then, the region has been one of near constant violence, with successive peace plans unable to stop the bloodshed. The latest, called a "road map for peace," has a hopeful world once again waiting and praying.

1949

Mao Proclaims the People's Republic of China

Mao Zedong was born in 1893 to a family that had once been peasants but had become fairly prosperous farmers and grain merchants. After years of work, school and military service, in a country that was in upheaval, he and 11 others formed the Chinese Communist party in 1921. Distrust with the Nationalists, led by Chiang Kai-shek, led to hostilities between the two groups, and Mao and his small band of adherents took to the wilderness, where they would remain for the next two decades. There, from remote outposts, he led a guerrilla war to spread communism, increasingly winning the hearts of nearly one hundred million peasants. By October 1949, the Communists had gained control of the land, and Mao established the People's Republic of China; the Nationalists fled to Taiwan. It was a severe blow to the democratic West; the U.S.S.R. immediately recognized the new government. Mao would remain in control of China until his death in 1976. During his reign a great amount of land was returned to the poor, but on the minus side, his severe Maoist ideology led to the deaths of tens of millions by execution and starvation during the misguided Great Leap Forward and the harrowing Cultural Revolution.

Above, Chairman Mao at the ceremony announcing the People's Republic, October 1, 1949; at left, on horseback in 1947

Weddings

"With this ring I thee wed." These familiar, beautifully simple words have launched the union of many a couple, but few nuptials have matched the firepower of these half dozen hitchings. For some, like La Liz, well, she enjoyed it so much she just kept on doing it. For the Duke of Windsor, on the other hand, it meant kissing a crown goodbye. And as for Teddy Roosevelt . . . the old Rough Rider even had to horn in on his daughter's wedding picture.

1906

Nicholas Longworth and Alice Roosevelt, with President Theodore Roosevelt, The White House

Brown Brothers

1937

Wallis Warfield Simpson and the Duke of Windsor, Tours, France

AP

1956

Howell Conant

Grace Kelly (and Prince Rainier), Monaco

1959

**Prince Akihito and
Michiko Shoda, Ise
Grand Shrine, Japan**

1964

Elizabeth Taylor and Richard Burton, Montreal (first of two)

1981

**Prince Charles and
Princess Diana,
flanked by Prince
Edward, Queen
Elizabeth II and the
Queen Mother,
Buckingham Palace**

War in Korea

Late in the 15th century, Japan invaded Korea but was driven off. Four hundred years later, however, Japan finally managed to wrest control of the nation, and by 1910 annexed the Korean peninsula. After Japan was defeated in World War II, Allied troops held control of Korea below the 38th parallel, while the Soviets occupied North Korea. The U.S. turned the territorial dispute over to the United Nations, which was unable to make any headway. The cold war was in full swing, and Korea would end up paying a terrible price. On June 25, 1950, a rainy Sunday morning, North Korea, apparently with the approval of the Soviets, suddenly launched a massive attack. The U.N. Security Council voted to send in troops, which ended up being overwhelmingly American. Before long, China became involved on the side of the North Koreans, and for three years, characterized by humid summers and freezing winters, the hostilities played out until a truce finally called an end to the stalemate. More than two million Koreans were dead, another one million Chinese and nearly 37,000 American troops. Both North and South Korea were devastated, and millions were homeless. The land remains divided today. Ironically, Japan profited from the war: It was able to forge a resurgent industry, as it supplied U.N. forces with war materials.

U.S. Marines halted by a Chinese roadblock on December 15, 1950; below, a few months later, a child whose parents had recently been killed

1953

Forty-five million years ago, the Indian continent drifted northward and collided with Asia, forming a mountain range that would become the world's highest. At the top of these Himalayas is the majestic mount known as Everest. Prior to 1953, there had been several attempts to reach the 29,035-foot-high peak, but all had failed and more than a dozen lives were lost along the way. The feat was regarded by many as simply impossible, but on May 29, 1953, two men outdueled Everest and its avalanches, freezing temperatures and thoughtless winds. Climbing with a British expedition were a Sherpa called Tenzing Norgay and a beekeeper from New Zealand by name of Edmund Hillary, and together they redefined what was possible. As they neared the top of their ascent, they had to force themselves onward. Then, Hillary said later, in an interview with LIFE's Robert Sullivan, "You couldn't really see exactly where the top was. We couldn't find the summit . . . Up above us the snow rounded off into a dome, and we realized that that must be the top. It's not a really sharp summit—the sort you hold your hands around. It's a summit that you can stand on reasonably comfortably. Six or eight people could probably all stand together. A nice summit."

Below, the view from near the summit; above, Hillary and Norgay enjoying a cup of hot tea with lemon

Royal Geographical Society

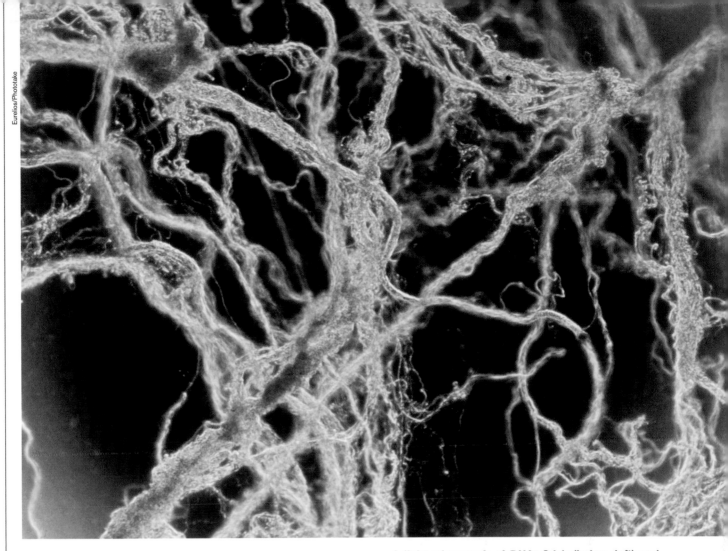

A light micrograph of DNA; Crick (below, left) and Watson in 1953, shortly after their "pretty" discovery

By 1943, scientists had identified deoxyribonucleic acid (DNA) as the molecule that carries genetic information. However, its structure remained elusive as researchers struggled to discover how this mysterious substance could convey its message from generation to generation. In 1952, British scientist Dr. Rosalind Franklin used new X-ray technology to produce images of DNA. A colleague of Franklin's showed an X-ray sub rosa to molecular biologists James Watson and Francis Crick. It confirmed their hypothesis that DNA consists of two chains of nucleotides zippered together. That parallel structure enables DNA to replicate itself. "We have found the secret of life," Crick announced. Its elegance was astounding, a ladder delicately twisting into a double helix, packing into a single, efficient strand all the information necessary to create a living being. "Could it really be this pretty? . . . we realized it probably was true because it was so pretty," said Watson. In April 1953 they published their findings, which fit the experimental data so perfectly their conclusion was almost immediately accepted. This discovery—one of the most significant of the 20th century—has pioneered new methods of treating diseases and unlocked the secrets of the human genome.

1953

The Double Helix

Carl Iwasaki

Linda (left) and Terry Lynn Brown making their way to the bus that will transport them to school

Brown v. Board of Education

Each morning, eight-year-old Linda Brown had to negotiate the hazardous terrain of a railroad yard to catch a bus to a school some 25 blocks away. Segregation in Topeka, Kan., prevented her from attending the all-white facility a few blocks from her house. In 1951 her parents, along with 12 other families, sued the Topeka Board of Education, demanding an end to racial separation. Because Linda came first alphabetically, she became the namesake for the litigation. Shepherded by an NAACP team, the case took three years to wend its way to the Supreme Court. In one of the far-reaching rulings of the century, the court found segregation in public schools unconstitutional. The unanimous decision proclaimed that "in the field of public education the doctrine of 'separate but equal' has no place." However, the victory was far from won as southern politicians vowed to defy the ruling. "The South will not abide by nor obey this legislative decision by a political court," said Senator James O. Eastland of Mississippi. The battle lines were drawn for the nation's long civil rights struggle.

Ross Madden

Salk's Polio Vaccine

Jonas Salk was born in New York City to Russian immigrants in 1914. Two years later, more than 2,000 people died of poliomyelitis there. The specter of the deadly scourge hung over the summers of his youth and into his adulthood, as public officials desperately tried to contain the paralyzing affliction by closing public pools and movie theaters. In 1947, Salk began researching the disease at the University of Pittsburgh School of Medicine. He discovered that an injection of the dead poliovirus stimulated the body's immune response without causing an infection. In 1954 he began human trials, and the public thrilled to hear of their success a year later. The results were profound, as getting the shots became a part of growing up, and four million were inoculated the first year the vaccine was available. By 1957, the number of new polio cases had been slashed dramatically, and Salk was a national hero who refused profits by declining to patent his medicine. Today the illness is virtually nonexistent in developed countries, and with improved versions of the vaccine, the World Health Organization has set its sights on eradicating polio by the end of 2005.

A new coming-of-age event– lining up for shots, April 1955

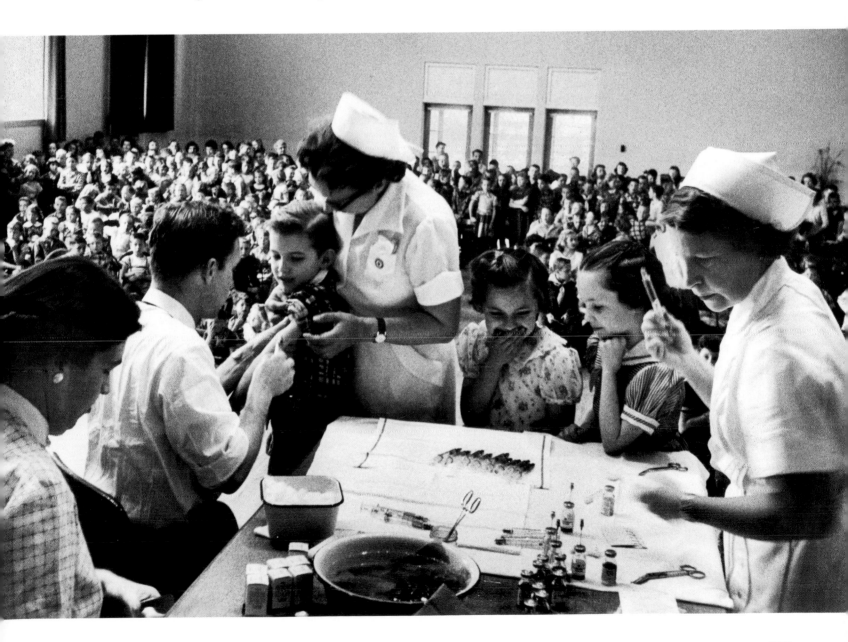

McDonald's
1955

Richard and Maurice McDonald, two brothers from New Hampshire, having failed to break into the movie business in California, eventually entered another unassailably American industry: the hamburger stand. BUY 'EM BY THE BAG, urged the sign advertising 15-cent patties at their San Bernardino store. They served only the holy trio—burgers, shakes and fries—but motorists flocked to their drive-thru because it was fast, cheap and reliable. One Illinois salesman, Ray Kroc, was so impressed that he bought franchise rights from the brothers in 1954, and opened his first store the next year. Five years later, he had a chain of more than 200 clones, each with a high-tech kitchen full of gadgets to ensure that every sandwich or bag of fries was exactly the same. His zeal for standardization dictated how the customers were greeted, the potatoes fried and the floors mopped. After buying the McDonalds out in 1961, Kroc then sold franchising rights to others, provided they received their Bachelor of Hamburgerology, with a minor in french fries, from Hamburger University, now in Oak Brook, Ill. People worldwide have developed a taste for these inexpensive, and some say sinfully unhealthy, burgers, and the Golden Arches gleam over towns from Bangalore to Bangor.

The McDonald's museum at the site of Kroc's first store, Des Plaines, Iowa

Disneyland

1955

When the greatest of all amusement parks opened in Anaheim, Calif., in July 1955, it was a great big disaster. Temperatures climbed to 110° and a plumbers' strike caused water fountains to run dry. Walt Disney had already invested $17 million in his 160-acre theme park, but it wasn't enough to keep Fantasyland from losing power and thousands of entrants from flooding in with fake tickets. It was such a debacle that Disney referred to opening day as Black Sunday. But he was determined to keep his dream alive, and less than two months later, the park welcomed its one millionth visitor. The celebrated animator had successfully built a land where everyone, adults included, could play in Sleeping Beauty Castle, romp with Mickey Mouse or scream their way down a Swiss mountain on a gleaming new roller coaster. Disney had hoped it would "be a source of joy and inspiration to all the world," and with the addition of sites in Florida, Tokyo, Paris and Hong Kong, his wish has been granted.

Below, Disney and the park's first guests; at left, Sleeping Beauty Castle in July 1955

Elvis Appears on
The Ed Sullivan Show

Four out of every five TV sets in America were tuned in to the show. If you were a young guy, and remotely hip, you were watching. If you were a young gal, no matter what, you were watching. If you were an adult, you watched it in the same way that you can't avert your eyes from a bus crash. There had never been anything quite like him. Elvis had been on television a few times before, but on September 9, 1956, he was on *The Ed Sullivan Show,* it was Sunday night, and America would never be the same. He sang both sides of his monster single "Don't Be Cruel" and "Hound Dog," and introduced the title song of his first movie, *Love Me Tender.* He also did a cover of Little Richard's "Reddy Teddy." The 21-year-old Elvis was paid 50 grand, then a royal sum, for three appearances on *Sullivan.* By the third show, in January of '57, the message had gotten through: A worried CBS network decreed that Elvis be shot only from the waist up. The other stuff, down there, was too much.

Above, with the *Ed Sullivan* audience; at left, working the crowd at the Municipal Auditorium in New Orleans, August 12, 1956.

Sputnik

It was as though a huge, terrifying comet had suddenly streaked across our sky. On October 4, 1957, the Soviet Union launched a satellite into space that would pass over the earth more than 15 times a day for three months. It was only the size of a beach ball, but it weighed 184 pounds and emitted a steady beep that lasted a third of a second. Amateur radio operators could hear the beep, and if you weren't one of those, they played it for you on the TV and radio news. On certain days you could even see it with the naked eye. Americans were stunned. Obviously this thing was harmless, but everybody knew the Soviets might have sent up a nuclear weapon—or something. Doubts were cast over the whole of our educational system. Said the chancellor of the University of Kansas, "The little satellite says that our schools are no longer a luxury but are as important as the food we eat." Rocket scientist Wernher von Braun went further: "The Soviet's progress in space is frightening." Nobody in the U.S. of A. doubted that. The space race had begun, in earnest. The bad news is, a month later the Soviets sent up Sputnik 2! It weighed 1,120 pounds and carried a dog named Laika, the first space traveler.

Above, a ham radio operator and his wife listening to Sputnik on October 5 in Elm Grove, Wis.; at left, the satellite

Castro
Takes Command

In 1952 a young lawyer named Fidel Castro was preparing to run for Cuba's parliament, but his campaign was cut short when former president General Fulgencio Batista staged a coup and canceled the elections. Castro unsuccessfully challenged the regime in court, then vowed to overthrow Batista. After a bloody failure in 1953, Castro eventually gathered Cuban exiles from Mexico and led an expedition against Batista in 1956. Initially bested, Castro's followers went into the mountains, where they fought a guerrilla war and drew support by vowing to restore the constitution, respect civil liberties, and enact moderate reforms. However, shortly after Batista fled the country, these promises evaporated. The U.S. watched warily as the new leader organized the first communist country in the Western Hemisphere, pursuing radical policies of property redistribution and nationalization. Castro's fierce anti-American rhetoric and cozy friendship with the Soviets strained relations between the two nations, leading to a botched U.S.-backed coup at the Bay of Pigs. Dealings between the countries remain chilly, but Castro has persisted. He is now the longest-serving leader of any country in the world.

Fidel Castro on a political tour, January 1959

Ancient Skull Found by Leakeys

1959

With her pet Dalmatians bounding along beside her, British archaeologist Mary Douglas Leakey was scrambling over the rocks in Olduvai Gorge in northern Tanzania when she noticed a piece of thick bone protruding from the ground. It turned out to be part of a hominid skull. Her discovery, splashed over the pages of *National Geographic,* would dramatically redraw the human family tree and make Leakey and her husband, Louis, international celebrities. First, the find proved that mankind originated in Africa, not Asia (as was previously thought). Then Louis pushed back human history by announcing the skull was 600,000 years old, which would make it the oldest remains to date. Later tests, however, revealed that Louis had underestimated the antiquity of the discovery. The bones were actually 1.75 million years old, which meant humans had been around significantly longer than everyone had considered possible. The Leakeys' son Richard, an archaeologist who accompanied his parents on digs, reflected: "To me it's a question of being able to look backward and give the present a root . . . To give meaning to where we are today, we need to look at where we've come from."

Mary and Louis Leakey and their 11-year-old son, Philip, digging at the Olduvai Gorge site in Tanzania

Courtesy of Robert F. Sisson/National Geographic Society/Simon & Schuster

Assassinations

"Assassination is the extreme form of censorship," wrote George Bernard Shaw. If so, then the extreme censorship of a leading public figure makes for the most jolting of events. There have been all too many during the last 100 years. These are among the most memorable.

1948

Nonviolent Indian leader Mahatma Gandhi lies in state in New Delhi. He was killed on January 30 by Nathuram Vinayak Godse, a Hindu fanatic.

1963

Commuters on a New York train read the shocking news about the November 22 slaying of President John F. Kennedy, allegedly by Lee Harvey Oswald.

1968

In Atlanta, Coretta Scott King mourns her husband, Rev. Martin Luther King Jr., who was killed by sniper James Earl Ray on April 4.

1968

John F. Kennedy Jr. (center) is among the clan's children at a St. Patrick's Cathedral service in New York for his uncle Bobby, who was shot on June 5 by a Palestinian immigrant named Sirhan Sirhan. RFK had just won his fifth of six primaries in a presidential bid.

1980

Crowds pay final respects to rock legend John Lennon outside the Dakota building in New York City, where he was cut down on December 8 by Mark David Chapman.

Egyptian President Anwar Sadat is shot and killed by Muslim extremists in Cairo on October 6.

1981

The U-2 Incident

Pilot Francis Gary Powers was gliding along the atmosphere's edge on May 1, snapping pictures of Soviet military installations 80,000 feet below as part of a clandestine CIA operation, when his surveillance plane mysteriously crashed to earth. Unable to hit the self-destruct button, he found himself in the wreckage of his top-secret U-2 surrounded by KGB agents. The timing couldn't have been worse. The United States and the Soviet Union were heading into a Big Four summit meeting with high hopes of reaching an arms reduction deal. President Dwight D. Eisenhower scrambled to disavow the mission while Premier Nikita Khrushchev shot back with fiery rhetoric about broken trust. Unable to maintain the ruse that Powers had been studying weather patterns, the U.S. was forced to admit it was spying. A week's worth of attempts to revive the summit failed, leaving the cold war yet icier. Powers received a 10-year sentence, but returned home nearly two years later in a prisoner swap. There was no hero's welcome despite the fact he never divulged any details of the mission. Reflecting on Powers' courage, one military official remarked, "The mind still boggles [over] what we asked this man to do: Fly in a plane . . . over downtown Moscow, alone, unarmed and unafraid."

Francis Gary Powers; right, on trial in Moscow, August 18, 1960

Carl Mydans

Bettmann/Corbis

The Pill
1960

Dr. John Rock seemed an unlikely advocate for an oral contraceptive. At age 70, he was a devout Roman Catholic and an eminent physician known for treating infertility. But having seen the sometimes disastrous results of unwanted pregnancies, he agreed to help test the efficacy of a pill combining two female hormones to prevent ovulation. It was the largest drug trial to date, and highly successful. However, the Federal Drug Administration sat on the application from Searle, the original manufacturer, so Rock went to Washington to defend his work against allegations that the drug caused cancer and to allay moral and religious qualms. In response—he called the FDA representative "young man"—Rock stated, "I have been treating patients my entire life and you have no idea how wrong you are." In 1960, the drug won approval, and Enovid, the first birth-control pill, went on the market. Its popularity astounded even its manufacturers; in less than two years, more than a million women were using it. In its 45 years on the market, this oral contraceptive has proved simple, safe and almost 100 percent effective. It's the most prescribed medicine on the planet—so ubiquitous it is known simply as the Pill.

The Ortho Dialpak dispenser, 1963

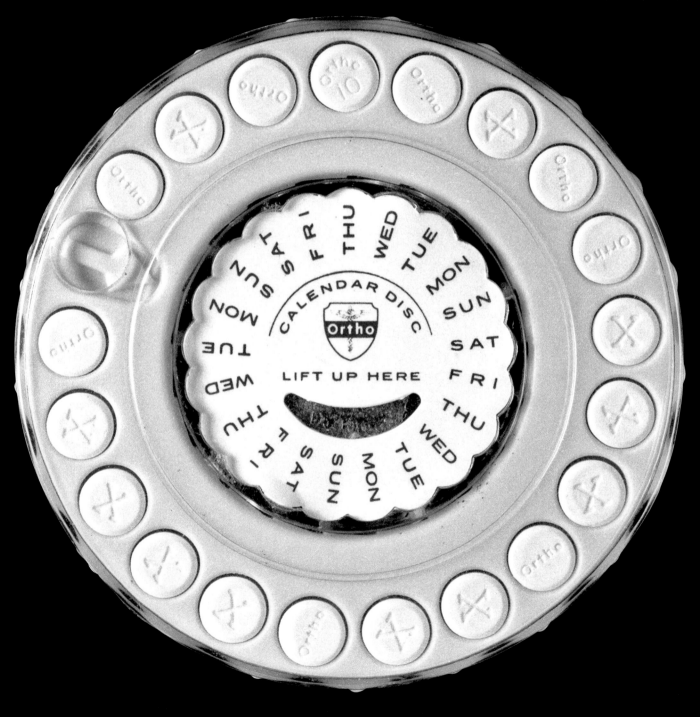

**Maiman with his apparatus,
July 1960**

The Laser

1960

Theodore Maiman, an American engineer working at a research lab in Malibu, Calif., created the first laser in 1960 using a rod fashioned from a ruby crystal encased in a high-intensity lamp. The lamp agitated the electrons of the crystal's atoms, making each one a kind of Mexican jumping bean. As the electrons lost energy, they simultaneously tumbled into their original state, and the freed energy took the form of light. Maiman harnessed that light, producing an intense beam that stayed focused even as it traveled away from its source. The invention was exciting for physicists who had been trying to prove a 1916 theory by Albert Einstein about photon emissions. The question now was what to do with this strange new device. It was dubbed "a solution looking for a problem." But over time, a plethora of uses have been revealed. Because the laser beam doesn't diffuse, it can be used for extremely precise work, guiding everything from giant drilling machines to delicate surgical instruments. Lasers are responsible for the clarity of sound produced by a CD, the sharpness of a page printed by a laser printer and the accuracy of information beamed from as far away as the moon.

Bettmann/Corbis

Four-year-old Brett Neilson blowing on a dandelion, 1965

Thalidomide

1961

An Australian physician named William McBride knew something was horribly wrong in 1961 when he delivered three babies, all of whom bore a rare birth defect. The infants' limbs were so short it seemed their hands and/or feet sprang directly from their bodies; their bowel systems were also malformed. McBride searched the mothers' medical records and discovered that to alleviate morning sickness they had all taken a new drug called thalidomide. He sent a letter to a medical journal outlining his concerns. Dr. Widukind Lenz, who had observed high rates of birth defects in Germany, shared McBride's theory that the problems were linked to the sedative and called the drug's German manufacturer, Chemie Grünenthal, warning of his findings. In the face of mounting bad press, the company took it off the market. Manufacturers in Great Britain, Canada and other countries followed suit, while in America, where the drug had not been released for commercial use, the FDA refused to approve it. By 1962 thalidomide was banned worldwide, but it was too late for some 20,000 children, many of whom never made it to their first birthday. Subsequent investigations pointed to an inadequate trial procedure, which led to the stiffening of drug-testing standards.

After the Sputnik shocker, NASA was propelled into a mean, fast game of catch-up. Then, on April 12, 1961, the Soviets dropped another space-race bombshell when they announced they had put a man into orbit and brought him back safely. The chosen pilot, Yuri Gagarin, had defied gravity in a five-ton craft that rocketed from the earth's surface and barreled around the globe as its inhabitant floated weightless inside. His 108-minute flight took Gagarin almost 200 miles high. There he observed the golden light along the horizon, bleeding into a black sky resplendent with stars. When the cosmonaut touched down it was to a national ovation, and Soviet citizens flooded Red Square to honor him. Premier Khrushchev congratulated him, saying, "You have made yourself immortal, because you are the first to penetrate into space." Back in the States, meanwhile, the mood was positively glum, and President Kennedy had to find some words to soothe a bested nation. So the young chief executive brashly vowed to put a man on the moon by decade's end, and the race went still faster.

Posters of Yuri Gagarin, Moscow, April 1961

James Whitmore

Andy Warhol

1962

As a commercial artist in the 1950s, Andy Warhol (né Warhola), the Pennsylvanian-born son of Czech immigrants, brought new ideas to the medium and enjoyed considerable success. From the beginning, however, as Calvin Tomkins wrote in *The New Yorker,* "he pursued fame with the single-mindedness of a spawning salmon." By the early '60s, the art world was bubbling with new ideas. Pop art was one of them. Warhol didn't invent pop art, but with an exhibition in 1962 at the Ferus Gallery in Los Angeles, he wowed 'em with his 32 canvases of Campbell's soup cans, one for each type the company made. This was really different. Warhol sold all of them. The problem was, he couldn't make them fast enough, so he turned to silk-screening, which made possible multiple, similar reproductions. He would never abandon the technique, generating memorable images of Marilyn Monroe, Mao, Hammer and Sickles, and Elvis. Perhaps his work was a commentary on society, the absurdity of it, the sameness, the disposability quotient. Warhol certainly wasn't going to say. "Art?" he said. "That's a man's name." But with his paintings, his movies (though they didn't move much), his *Interview* magazine, his passel of ever-so-hip acolytes and a magnificent talent for self-promotion, Andy Warhol changed the face of art.

***Orange Marilyn,* 1962; opposite, at The Factory, his New York City studio**

"It was a spring without voices. On the mornings that had once throbbed with the dawn chorus of robins . . . there was now no sound . . . No witchcraft, no enemy action had silenced the rebirth of new life in this stricken world. The people had done it themselves," wrote Rachel Carson in *Silent Spring,* her clarion call to a world besotted with caustic pesticides. The unassuming marine biologist from Pennsylvania demonstrated that, more than simply killing insects, DDT infiltrated the ecosystem, poisoning birds, robbing salmon of sustenance and eventually endangering humans. Her writing was clear and compelling, and the book became a surprise must-read that enjoyed 31 weeks on *The New York Times* Best Sellers list. Devotees flooded the Department of Agriculture with letters, prompting President John F. Kennedy to demand an investigation into pesticides. The results vindicated Carson, who had been denounced by some as a hysterical spinster. A slew of federal laws to protect the earth were passed, including a ban on DDT. *Silent Spring* was crucial to the evolution of the modern environmental movement. It was no longer possible to deny that "man, too, is part of this balance."

Alfred Eisenstaedt

1962

The First Wal-Mart

The son of a hardworking mortgage broker, Sam Walton was born in Kingfisher, Okla., in 1918. After serving in the war, he worked in retail, in a variety of roles. Often this kept him on the road, where he observed that the large chains inevitably placed their stores near population centers. Walton, however, "thought that larger stores could be put in smaller towns than anyone had tried before. There was a lot more business in those towns than people ever thought." Obviously, he was right. In 1962 he opened Wal-Mart Discount City in Rogers, Ark. Things started off slowly, but by 1970 there were 25 such stores. Today, Wal-Mart is the largest company in the world. One hundred million people shop at Wal-Mart's 3,400 American stores every week. Around the world, more than a million and a half people work for Wal-Mart. Sam Walton's approach was simple: He charged less than everybody else. He continually prowled competitors' outlets—and lowered his prices accordingly. Wal-Mart is one of the shining examples in the history of capitalism. Wal-Mart also has incurred charges that it crushes businesses and alters the personalities of small towns the country over, and is increasingly the target of litigation ranging from sex discrimination to wage and pay disputes.

Grand reopening of original Wal-Mart, Rogers, Ark., 1973; sixth adult from right: Sam Walton

Cuban Missile Crisis

1962

When President Kennedy learned the Soviets had ballistic missiles in Cuba—a scant 90 miles off the U.S. coast—that could be fitted with nuclear warheads, he had to make a tough decision. Proceed diplomatically? Give the order for air strikes on the Caribbean island nation? Kennedy's Secretary of Defense, Robert McNamara, cautioned, "I don't know quite what kind of a world we'll live in after we've struck Cuba. How do we stop at that point?" On October 22, the President decided on a naval blockade to halt the military buildup. Two days later Soviet ships reached the quarantine line, while the opposing sides testily eyed each other. Without any question, the two superpowers hovered on the edge of war. As McNamara later said, "We literally looked down the gun barrel into nuclear war." Finally, on October 28, Khrushchev blinked, and agreed to dismantle the bases in exchange for Kennedy's promise not to invade Cuba. "It was luck that prevented nuclear war," McNamara reflected. "Rational individuals came that close to total destruction of their societies . . . the major lesson of the Cuban missile crisis is this: the indefinite combination of human fallibility and nuclear weapons will destroy nations."

The Profumo Scandal

The cold war was in a deep freeze and swingin' London had not yet blossomed when British Prime Minister Harold Macmillan's government was rocked by a political scandal seething with steamy sexuality. The episode began in 1961 when ultra-Tory John Dennis Profumo, Macmillan's secretary of war, met a show-girl and occasional prostitute named Christine Keeler at a pool party at Lord Astor's country mansion organized by osteopath-socialite Stephen Ward. Profumo and the 19-year-old Keeler had a torrid affair, that, although brief, attracted a certain amount of attention. None of this might have mattered but it emerged that Keeler was also having an affair with the naval attaché at the Soviet embassy. Profumo might still have escaped from the controversy, but he stated in the House of Commons in March 1963 that there had been "no impropriety whatever" in his relationship with Keeler. Fleet Street was having a field day with the entire matter, which included rumors of wild sex parties with two-way mirrors and evenings at which a reputed cabinet member served dinner wearing nothing but a mask. With scads of evidence about, Profumo confessed in June that he had misled the House, and resigned. Charged with pandering, Ward later killed himself. In October, Macmillan himself resigned, claiming poor health.

Getty

Above, Christine Keeler, June 6, 1963; at right, 12 days later, John Profumo with his wife, the noted actress Valerie Hobson

Bettmann/Corbis

President Johnson signing the Civil Rights Act in Washington, D.C.

President Lyndon B. Johnson knew how to bully and cajole a bill through the Senate, but this was a different matter. The marathon filibuster to block the Civil Rights Act was approaching its 75th day, with no end in sight. On-the-fence senators wondered if the legislation was necessary. Then, a tragedy unexpectedly handed Johnson an important weapon. Three young civil rights workers had gone missing in rural Mississippi, their burned-out car found just off the highway. Fearing violence would escalate if the bill didn't pass, the previously undecided swung toward Johnson and shattered the filibuster. On July 2, 1964, LBJ signed the Civil Rights Act, a comprehensive bill banning, among other things, segregation in restaurants, hotels and other public places. It also forbade employment discrimination on the basis of race and, because of a last-minute blunder by a conservative congressman, gender. To a nation torn by racial strife, the act meant the federal government now stood resolutely behind the fight to end inequality. "Let us close the springs of racial poison," Johnson declared, but he hadn't closed them fast enough for the three missing men. Their bodies were discovered five weeks later. They had been killed by Klansmen and buried in a muddy dam.

1964

Congress Passes Civil Rights Act

The Beatles Invade America

By the year 1964, virtually all the fizz had gone out of rock 'n' roll. Since his discharge from the Army a few years earlier, Elvis was a shadow of his former self, and fellow pioneers Chuck Berry and Jerry Lee Lewis had problems of their own. Further, America was still on its heels after the shocking assassination of the President in November of '63. Then on February 7, 1964, the dei ex machina arrived by airplane at New York's Kennedy Airport to a crowd of thousands of screaming kids. Hailing from Liverpool, England, John Lennon, Paul McCartney, George Harrison and Ringo Starr had the clothes, hair and accents to make them irrepressibly fresh, but they also were more clever and more talented than any other pop music group in history. When they appeared on Ed Sullivan's show two days later the result was pandemonium, which only continued to spread as the Fab Four produced one brilliant hit after another, in a series that wound its way through remarkably inventive musical approaches. At the beginning, young people emulated their look. Before long, the Beatles had become rock gurus for millions of youths around the world who listened to their latest offerings as if they were cultural messages from above. Of course, it had to come to an end, and irresolvable tensions forced the lads to break up. They all went on to successful solo careers, but there would never be anything again like the Beatles.

From top, George, John, Paul and Ringo, Kennedy Airport, New York, February 1964

Curt Gunther/London Features

Fashion

"Fashion is something barbarous, for it produces innovation without reason and imitation without benefit." So said philosopher George Santayana, who apparently had no sense of line, texture or visual drama. Innovations in attire—sometimes jaw-dropping—have given society some of its biggest surprises over the last 100 years.

Underwood & Underwood/Corbis

1926

In December, flappers show off their style high atop Chicago's Sherman Hotel.

A crowd in San Francisco takes its first look at a new synthetic fiber. In May 1940, lines formed as the first nylon stockings reached the stores.

1939

Dupont Company

c. 1940

Conde Nast Archive/Corbis

Russian ballerina Irina Baronova is delightedly *en pointe* in her narrow-trousered harlequin lounging pajamas and bare-midriff blouse.

1946

Marilyn Monroe sports a new approach to sun 'n' fun: the bikini.

1966

The miniskirt first popped in London, but quickly found its way to the streets of New York City.

1993

The noted fashion columnist Eugenia Sheppard once said, "To call a fashion wearable is the kiss of death." Oh, that explains why supermodel Naomi Campbell is taking this tumble on a Paris runway.

First U.S. Ground Forces Sent to Vietnam

Following the Japanese surrender in World War II, Communists and Nationalists led by Ho Chi Minh declared that Vietnam, which had been controlled by France for six decades, was now an independent state. The French demurred, leading to fighting that ended badly for them in 1954. A Geneva conference then decreed that Vietnam would be ruled by Communists in the North, while the South would be nominally democratic. Before too long, insurgencies in the South, supported by the North, led the U.S. to worry that communism might extend its tentacles yet farther. So aid and advisers were dispatched, to the extent that by August 1964, there were 16,000 American "advisers" in place—a lot of personnel, granted, but it was something far, far away. That all changed on March 8, 1965, when two battalions of Marines landed on beaches near Da Nang. Within three years, there would be half a million U.S. troops there. When Saigon finally fell to the Communist forces in April 1975, U.S. casualties had exceeded 200,000. The war ravaged Vietnam and nearly tore the heart out of America, as generations squared off in noisy, vicious discord that at times seemed to threaten the very fiber of the nation. The bitterness felt on all sides across the country—not least by the underappreciated and often-damaged returning vets—lingers to this day.

On March 8, 1965, men from the 3rd Battalion, 9th Marines, landing on a beach 10 miles from Da Nang—the first U.S. troops in Vietnam

Israeli soldiers after recapturing the Western, or Wailing, Wall in Jerusalem

19**6**7 The Six-Day War

In the middle of 1967, Israel was in trouble. It was cut off from its oil supply by an Egyptian blockade of the Gulf of Aqaba; harassed by border raids from Syria; and unable to secure protection from its allies. Israel responded with a startling preemptive strike on the Egyptian air force, demolishing in three hours the majority of Egypt's planes and air bases. Six days later, the Star of David flew over the Gaza Strip, the Sinai Peninsula, the Golan Heights and the West Bank of the Jordan. The Six-Day War—known to the Arab world as The Setback—was nothing short of a rout, acomplished by a masterly set of military tactics, and the world was stunned by the prowess of this young nation. Jews rushed into the now-united city of Jerusalem, while the Arabs licked their wounds. With their armies in shambles, Arab states began financing the Palestine Liberation Organization.

Barnard Performs First Heart Transplant

Ralph Waldo Emerson counsels us to make friendship from "the tough fibre of the human heart." The world got to witness the resilience of those fibers on December 3, 1967, when Dr. Christiaan Barnard performed the first heart transplant, in Cape Town, South Africa. After carefully lifting brain-dead Denise Darvall's healthy heart from her chest, Barnard's surgical team painstakingly attached it to the veins and arteries in the cavity that had held Louis Washkansky's dying one. The surgeons then applied an electrical charge to the transplanted organ, which leapt with the shock and began swiftly beating. "Christ, it's going to work!" cried Barnard. The organ did its job for 18 days, residing uneasily at first in the space left by Washkansky's enlarged heart, until the patient eventually succumbed to a lung infection. The new heart, however, had stayed strong until the end. Barnard's next transplant recipient lived 19 months after the operation, and his sixth survived for 24 years. Transplant technology has developed since that first procedure, with increasing rates of success and longer lives for the donees.

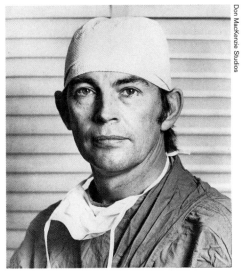

Don MacKenzie Studios

Below, patient Washkansky with nurse and Dr. Barnard, Cape Town, December, 1967

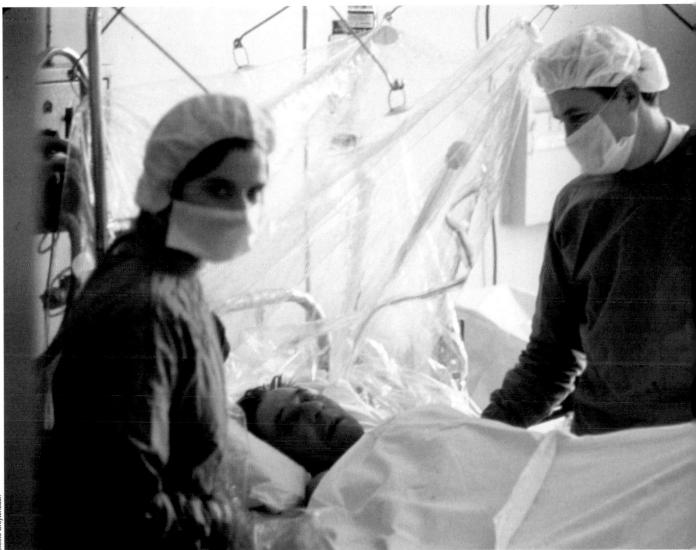

David Newell Smith/The Observer/Getty

Cloete Breytenbach

Muhammad Ali Refuses to Enter Draft

1967

At age 25, heavyweight boxing champion Muhammad Ali was still the wiseacre kid, brimming with quick-witted boasts delivered in high bombast, accompanied by a taunting, lightning-handed boxing style that had opponents baffled and spectators agape. But when on April 28, 1967, he refused to register for the draft on the basis of his Muslim faith, the world saw a more serious side of the Champ. He declared, "I cannot be true to my belief in my religion by accepting such a call." After that, he would never be just a boxer again. Opinions varied: He was a shame to his race; a hero; a misguided naïf; a man of conscience. The World Boxing Association stripped him of his title, and Ali spent three years appealing his conviction for draft evasion, eventually winning. In 1974, he vanquished George Foreman in the Rumble in the Jungle to reclaim the crown. Over time, the rancor caused by his draft refusal mostly melted away. In 1996, three billion watched as Ali, trembling with Parkinson's but indomitable still, lighted the Olympic torch in Atlanta. *Paris Review* editor George Plimpton observed, "They would marvel that through the wonderful excesses of skill and character, he had become the most famous athlete, indeed, the best-known personage in the world."

Olympic Black Power Salute

At the 1968 Summer Olympics in Mexico City, Tommie Smith ran the 200-meter dash in 19.83 seconds, shattering the world record. As he walked off the field with his teammate John Carlos, who had just won the bronze, Smith was not about to celebrate their victories. This son of an African American sharecropper had lived through years of poverty and abuse picking cotton in Texas. He had heard the news of four black girls who were killed in a Birmingham church the year he entered college, and had been moved by the assassination of Martin Luther King Jr. that April. "This is it, man," Smith said to Carlos, "All those years of fear, all the suffering. This is it." The two donned black gloves, then removed their shoes to represent poverty. Smith wore a black scarf and Carlos wore beads to symbolize lynching. When the national anthem began, the sprinters raised their fists and the spectators responded with both cheers and boos. Within 48 hours, the International Olympic Committee ruled to dismiss the entire U.S. contingent if the two men were not punished; so they were suspended and sent home, where they received death threats. Smith's record stood for almost 11 years, but his raised fist is still seared into the world's memory.

October 16, 1968, left to right, Australian Peter Norman, Smith, Carlos

Ken Regan

Arthur Shay

1968

Riots at the Chicago Convention

Chicago, that City of Big Shoulders, has been home to more political conventions than any other place in America. In 1860 the Republican party convened there and selected Abraham Lincoln as its candidate. In 1932, Democrat Franklin D. Roosevelt showed up on the last night and, with the first acceptance speech ever, drummed up support for his New Deal. The affair the Democrats held in August of 1968 met with considerably less success. The climate in the country was one of utter turbulence. In recent months Robert Kennedy and Martin Luther King Jr. had been gunned down, while on the other side of the world young Americans were dying in an unpopular war. The antiwar movement targeted the convention, and 10,000 demonstrators took to the streets of Chicago. There they were met by May-

or Richard Daley's defense force: 11,900 police, 15,000 Army and National Guardsmen and 1,000 Secret Service agents. Daley was not going to permit the protestors to approach the convention center. The protestors wanted their message heard, and wouldn't cave in. The result, caught chillingly by network television cameras, was appalling violence in the streets as the police made vigorous use of tear gas while flailing right and left with their batons. Innocent bystanders and reporters were beaten. To be sure, a lot of these demonstrators weren't above mayhem of their own, but viewers across the land were sickened as the chant "The whole world is watching!" resounded again and again. It was a staggering blow to the Democrats, and Richard Nixon would go on to win the election.

Police moving through a tear-gas fog in Chicago's Lincoln Park

Man Walks on the Moon

In 1961, President John F. Kennedy stated that he wanted a man on the moon before the decade ended. After years of being outpaced by the seemingly indomitable Soviet program, NASA finally fulfilled JFK's dream when Neil Armstrong, Edwin "Buzz" Aldrin Jr. and Michael Collins climbed aboard *Apollo 11*. Their eight-day journey into space was a welcome relief from seemingly endless news feeds of urban riots and mounting Vietnam War casualties. On July 20, 1969, one sixth of the world's population—600 million people—were glued to their television sets as Armstrong and Aldrin bounced gracefully onto the moon, leaving footprints in the soft, lunar dust. It was Armstrong who touched down first, uttering those immortal, if somewhat inscrutable, words, "That's one small step for man, one giant leap for mankind." (He would later claim that static deleted the "a" before "man", obscuring the meaning.) Despite the fact that their mission was in part fueled by the cold war rivalry between two nations armed to the teeth with nuclear weapons, the message the astronauts left on the moon was serene: "We came in peace for all mankind."

Old Glory deployed by Armstrong, left, and Aldrin, July 20, 1969

NASA

1969

Woodstock

There was, beginning in the middle 1960s, a large counterculture in America made up of people under 30. There had been nothing like it before nor has there been since. By no means did all young people belong to this group, but a great many did, and they had certain, very specific things in common. Their hair was longer than the others', they experimented with drugs, they believed in free sex, they were against the war in Vietnam—and they were really into their rock music. They believed there had to be a better, more peaceful way to handle things than how their parents had. In August 1969, some 400,000 of them went to a pasture in Bethel, N.Y., to attend a concert featuring dozens of their rock idols. It had been planned to go off in Woodstock, not far away, but the site was changed, and dizzying traffic jams developed and a lot of folks had to walk for miles. Despite woefully inadequate facilities, torrential rain, demons in the sound system, waits as long as two hours between sets, and myriad other snafus, the show went on, and the kids amazed their elders by not rioting but rather getting along for three days. Implicit here was a message that maybe there was hope for a better world. That, however, guttered out a few months later after an ugly explosion of Hell's Angels violence at another big rock concert, this time called Altamont.

A youthful pilgrimage, Bethel, N.Y., August 1969

1970
Bangladesh Cyclone

The Ganges and the Brahmaputra rivers empty into the shallow Bay of Bengal with the crashing force of seven Mississippi Rivers, leaving silt that creates a low-slung archipelago. Here on these islands, farmers eke out an existence bounded by droughts and monsoons. On November 13, 1970, a powerful cyclone engorged the mighty rivers with rain, creating a 20-foot storm surge that obliterated the islanders' fragile dwellings. Some half a million people drowned in the churning waters, and cholera and typhoid beset survivors as an unstable government grappled with relief measures. World leaders responded with aid pledges, including President Richard Nixon, who promised $10 million. The news also struck a chord with former Beatle George Harrison, who organized some of his friends, including Bob Dylan, Eric Clapton and Ringo Starr, for two sold-out shows at Madison Square Garden. The concert not only established Harrison as a pioneering philanthropist but also paved the way for fund-raising shows like Live Aid, Farm Aid and the Tibetan Freedom Concert.

Travail wrought by the cyclone, November 1970

Watergate

At 2:30 a.m. on June 17, 1972, five men were arrested at Washington, D.C.'s plush Watergate Hotel after a security guard discovered them fine-tuning bugs they had planted in Democratic National Committee headquarters. One of the men was James W. McCord, security director for the Republican Party's Committee to Re-Elect the President. What evolved from this was grand opera with a Machiavellian overture, boasting a cast of provocative characters who became household names as the country's most notorious political scandal ever played out before an absorbed, and disturbed, national audience. *Washington Post* reporters Bob Woodward and Carl Bernstein doggedly followed every possible trail until finally they came up with a source at the FBI they

called Deep Throat, and with his help they traced a path leading directly to the White House. Nearly a year after the initial arrests, and a grand jury investigation, several key advisers to President Richard Nixon either resigned or were fired. In May 1973 Congressional hearings began, presided over by North Carolina Sen. Sam Ervin. Through the long summer, viewers watched as the stench of culpability drifted ever closer to the chief executive himself. The dagger to the heart came when it was revealed that Nixon had taped his Oval Office conversations. He tried everything to cover up his involvement in the seemingly mundane Watergate break-in, but in the end he was hoist with his own petard. The President of the United States was forced to resign on August 9, 1974.

Comm... ... ... **Baker**... ... ... **attorn**...

1973

Roe v. Wade

In 1973, two young lawyers, Sarah Weddington and Linda Coffee, initiated a class-action suit on behalf of an anonymous plaintiff, with the pseudonym Jane Roe, who wanted to terminate her pregnancy although Texas prohibited such abortions. The Dallas County District Attorney Henry Wade defended the law. When it went to the Supreme Court, neither party seemed up to pleading one of the most important cases of the century. The befuddled attorneys offered tepid arguments. After a second round—this time both sides were better prepared—Justice Harry Blackmun concluded that the 14th Amendment's implicit right to privacy protects a woman's decision whether or not to have an abortion. On January 22, six other justices joined Blackmun, and the Court handed down a sweeping ruling, overturning laws in 46 states. Antiabortion camps flooded Blackmun with letters, some so virulent that he was placed under federal protection. Polls at the time indicated that the public was about evenly split on the issue, and these numbers haven't changed much, as the debate rages ever on.

Washington, D.C., 1974

Dirck Halstead/Time

Christopher Springmann

1973

Oil Embargo

"Oil is like a wild animal. Whoever captures it has it," said oilman J. Paul Getty. In 1973, with American oil use outpacing domestic supply, the beast belonged to the Organization of Petroleum Exporting Countries, a cartel of mostly Arab nations that produced the majority of the world's fuel. Flexing their newly collectivized muscle, OPEC agreed in October to cut off supply to the United States and the Netherlands as punishment for their support of Israel. OPEC also raised prices across the board, charging up to 130 percent more by year's end. The effects were striking: lines at gas stations stretching for blocks and through-the-ceiling heating bills. The U.S. government imposed a nationwide speed limit of 55 mph, year-round Daylight Saving Time, and urged citizens to turn their thermostats down. (President Richard Nixon proclaimed that his doctor said keeping the house cooler was better for your health.) The drive for efficiency also changed auto manufacturing—gone were the massive gas-guzzling machines of the 1960s (at least for the time being). OPEC turned the tap back on in March 1974, but the effects—recession alternating with inflation—would be felt for years. The balance of global power had shifted slightly, as OPEC held at the ready its newfound weapon.

Waiting for gas, Palo Alto, Calif.

Robert Foothorap

1976

Apple II, the First Personal Computer

By the early 1970s, computers had come a long way since the abacus, but they remained large, ungainly, million-dollar machines, whirring through punch cards in obscure corners of research labs and Defense Department offices. Then two college dropouts, tinkering away in one of their parents' garages in Los Altos, Calif., developed a little device that would revolutionize the world. Twenty-five-year-old Steve Wozniak, inspired by Altair 8800, a microcomputer kit marketed to nerds who wanted to build their own, screwed a bunch of microchips onto a plank to make a prototype of the first computer intended for the everyday consumer. Wozniak showed it to his friend Steve Jobs, all of 21 years old and living with his parents. Together, the Steves would develop the Apple II, which came fully assembled and was easy to use. For seed money, Wozniak hocked his programmable calculator, and Jobs sold his Volkswagen minibus. Their expectations were low enough that Wozniak held on to his day job at Hewlett-Packard, but the Apple II was a runaway success. By 1987, computers were in 25 million homes, schools and offices, and the two former hippies were rich men.

Steve Wozniak (sitting) and Steve Jobs, October 1979

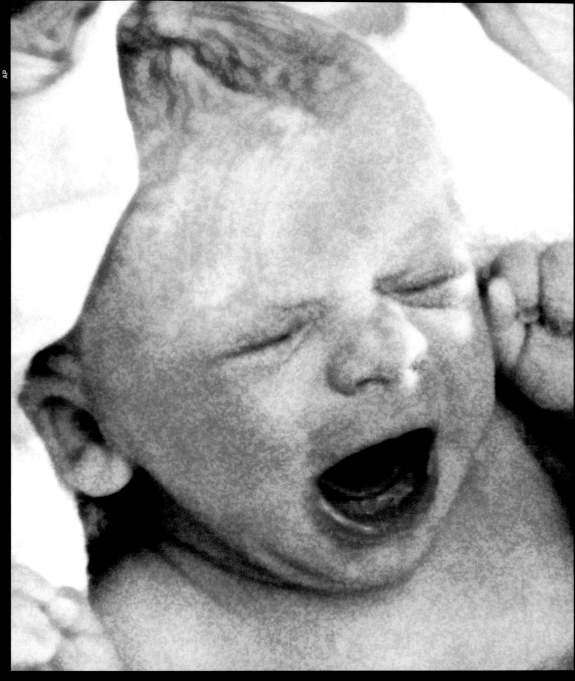

Louise Joy Brown, shortly after her birth in Oldham, England, on July 25, 1978

When Louise Brown came squalling into the world on July 25, 1978, to an exhausted mother and a jubilant father, she was by all accounts a typical baby—except that little Louise's cries were heard around the world. Her mother, Lesley, had been unable to become pregnant because of a defect in her fallopian tubes. So, in a technique that had taken 12 years to perfect, British medical researchers Patrick Steptoe and R.G. Edwards extracted an egg from Lesley's ovary, fertilized it with her husband's sperm and, as the cell that would become Louise began to divide, implanted it into Lesley's womb. The birth was the first of its kind and was acclaimed as a miracle of modern medicine. But to some it also presented an ethical dilemma about what constituted "natural" conception. Some Catholic officials expressed "grave misgivings" and a doctor who had attempted in vitro fertilization in the United States five years earlier was accused by his superiors of trying to "create a monstrosity in this world." Louise, however, defied any such concerns, growing into a darling toddler with blonde curls and blue eyes. Today there are more than a million people who began their lives as test-tube babies

The First Test-tube Baby

Three Mile Island

1979

The harnessing of nuclear energy has been one of the signature developments of the last 100 years. For many it is the equivalent of a genie in a bottle; for others, it is a Pandora's box. Early on March 28, 1979, at the Three Mile Island Nuclear Generating Station in the Susquehanna River in central Pennsylvania, not far from the capital city of Harrisburg, there was a frightening development. TMI is home to two nuclear reactors. On that day a condensate valve in Unit 2 suffered what was either a mechanical or an electrical failure, shutting off the water supply. The reactor core shut down automatically, but then a combination of equipment malfunctions, operator errors and bad decisions led to a crisis in which there was an eventual partial core meltdown. One unsettling month later, the core was finally cooling down. Some radioactive gas was released, although tests indicated the levels were not dangerous. There are area residents, however, who are convinced that radioactive harm was done. Unit 2 was sufficiently damaged that it will not be used again. Unit 1 reopened in 1985, and has a good record. Prior to the TMI accident, nuclear power plants were proliferating. There has not been a single one built in the U.S. since, although changes in training and other areas have led to an environment in which new facilities are in the initial-consideration phase.

Cooling towers at Three Mile Island

Space

"The American experience stirred mankind from discovery to exploration," said the former Librarian of Congress Daniel J. Boorstin. "From the cautious quest for what they knew (or thought they knew) was out there, into an enthusiastic reaching to the unknown. These are two substantially different kinds of human enterprise." Manned spacecraft have taught us about ourselves and the world around us. Unmanned explorations, like these, have brought the future into our present.

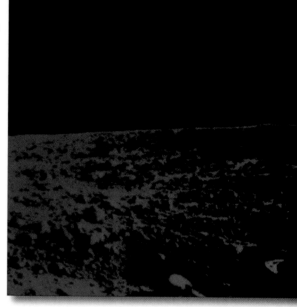

Viking was sent to investigate our neighbor Mars. Here, the sun is setting over the horizon of the Red Planet.

In this image from the Voyager spacecraft, the color variations represent the different compositions of Saturn's rings.

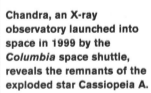

1999

The Hubble Space Telescope, which was launched in 1990, sent back this otherworldly glimpse of the Omega, or Swan Nebula, part of the constellation Sagittarius.

2004

Chandra, an X-ray observatory launched into space in 1999 by the *Columbia* space shuttle, reveals the remnants of the exploded star Cassiopeia A.

AIDS

In the summer of 1981, patients in New York City and Los Angeles began exhibiting a new and perplexing ailment: A war of attrition on their immune systems had left them unable to fight off certain infections and malignancies. By 1982, the condition had a name—Acquired Immunodeficiency Syndrome, or AIDS. Since the earliest cases were in gay men, a skittish media barely covered them. The federal government was reluctant to fund research, and some homophobic doctors theorized it was an allergic reaction to promiscuity. "This failure of the system leaves a legacy of unnecessary suffering that will haunt the Western world

for decades to come," wrote Randy Shilts in his groundbreaking book on AIDS, *And the Band Played On.* The disease was also closely linked to intravenous drug use. There were dedicated researchers who discovered that the disease was caused by a virus they called HIV, which rapidly mutates and has eluded attempts to find a vaccine. By the decade's end, AIDS had reached pandemic proportions, and the world could no longer pretend it was just a "gay cancer," but rather something that people from all walks of life were vulnerable to. Some 20 million have died of AIDS, and there is still no cure.

A hospital worker in Romania attending to a young AIDS victim, 1990

Madonna's *Like a Virgin*

Three decades after Elvis's gyrations set in motion a new era of raw, rock 'n' roll sexuality, a girl from outside of Detroit spilled out of a bustier on the cover of her second album, wearing a belt, its buckle emblazoned with the words BOY TOY. *Like a Virgin* made Madonna a pop icon and a symbol of frank, pragmatic female sexuality. Where Elvis begged "Don't be cruel," Madonna tossed off, "They can beg and they can plead, but they can't see the light, that's right." Folks who had frantically queued up for the newest Elvis platter watched bemusedly—and concernedly—as their kids did the same for *Like a Virgin,* which went platinum in a month. Songs like the title track and "Material Girl" were paragons of dance-pop with a post-punk sensibility that also dipped into African American rhythms. Her brash, sexy style was unforgettable—her racy trademark underwear-as-outerwear became a 1980s equivalent to Beatle boots as mallrats everywhere emulated her style. Over the years, Madonna has slithered through seemingly endless incarnations, each one closely watched and copied. After lustily kissing fellow pop star Britney Spears in 2003, she proved she still had the chutzpah to launch a thousand headlines.

Madonna performing
in Los Angeles on
The Virgin Tour, 1985

Challenger

1986

Early on the morning of January 28, 1986, millions of TV viewers watched Christa McAuliffe, a high school teacher from New Hampshire, give a wave from the tarmac in front of a giant spaceship. Astronauts had already been the stuff of legend, but here was McAuliffe, an ordinary woman, about to climb aboard the shuttle. If she could fly into space, maybe we all could. Just shy of 74 seconds after its flawless takeoff, *Challenger* suddenly burst into flames, and its debris crashed into the ocean, leaving but a scythe of smoke across the sky. That night, President Ronald Reagan tried to comfort a horrified nation: "The future doesn't belong to the fainthearted; it belongs to the brave. The *Challenger* crew was pulling us into the future, and we'll continue to follow them." In reality, the United States space program screeched to a halt, with no backup launching system and nagging questions about whether we really belonged up there in the first place. NASA eventually regained some momentum, but the parabolic descent of the shuttle was seared into the country's memory, echoing the lines of poet Rainer Maria Rilke—"Let the Archangel now . . . take a single step down and toward us: our own heart, beating on high would beat us down."

The explosion of the space shuttle *Challenger*, January 28, 1986

Chernobyl
1986

"Behold a pale horse: and his name that sat on him was Death, and Hell followed with him," says the Book of Revelation. But on April 26, 1986, Death rode a radioactive plume rising from a nuclear power plant in Chernobyl, Ukraine. Explosions during a safety test blew the roof off the reactor building and started fires that would rage for 12 days. Plant officials wanted to clear the area, but the government, scrambling to hide the disaster, refused, and residents placidly went about their routine under the ruddy glow. Moscow eventually approved the evacuation of more than 100,000 people, all the while insisting that the situation was under control. Crackling Geiger counters in Sweden, however, told a different story, and, as winds wafted the poison over Europe, fear and anger swept the continent. Eighteen days after the accident, Soviet leader Mikhail Gorbachev acknowledged the gravity of the situation, but the deed had been done. More than 31 people died in the blasts and another 4,000 perished in the aftermath, making it the worst reactor accident to date. Still today, the hell that followed rages, as elevated cancer rates reportedly plague the area, especially among children.

Below, a reactor cleaning team in 1986; at left, the abandoned town of Pripyat, not far from Chernobyl

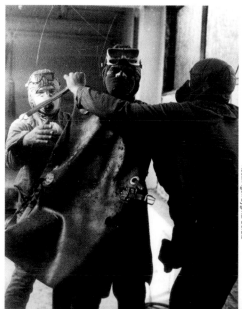

Tiananmen Square

One of the world's major plazas, Tiananmen Square was created in 1651 and today covers some 100 acres in the center of Beijing. Since 1919, Tiananmen has also been the site for student demonstrations. On June 5, 1989, the world watched as one of the great dramas of our time took place, starring man and machine. In April, rallies had begun for democratic reforms in the rigidly governed nation. Despite a declaration of martial law, students and workers continued to gather until more than a million people were in Tiananmen. Finally, on June 4, the ruling powers had had enough, and tanks were dispatched to clear the square. The conflict spread to adjoining streets, and hundreds of civilians were killed. The next day, Tiananmen lay quiet as a row of tanks slowly wheeled across the square. Suddenly a young man, armed only with what appeared to be his shopping bag, stepped in front of a tank. As the tank tried to go around him to the right, the man moved to his left; when the vehicle attempted to pass on the other side, the man simply stayed in front of it. Across China and the world, viewers watched with astonishment as the entire row of tanks was held in check by this one anonymous man. It was a stirring moment for humanity. After a half hour, someone emerged from the crowd and drew the man away; the tanks then continued on their way. The crackdown on the demonstrators was followed by the government's steadfast refusal to implement any changes. You could say all was for naught, but the point had been made: Courage carries its own distinction.

Stuart Franklin/Magnum (2)

At left, Tiananmen Square, May 26, 1989; above, man vs. machine, June 5

Exxon Valdez
Oil Spill

At 12:04 a.m. on March 24, 1989, the oil tanker *Exxon Valdez* smashed into a reef while maneuvering through the lattice of fjords in Alaska's pristine Prince William Sound. The vessel disgorged nearly 11 million gallons of its viscous cargo, trapping birds and mammals in a thick, heavy, black goo. Environmentalists had long warned of a catastrophe of this magnitude, but some oil execs brushed off these concerns, claiming that they were prepared for accidents of any size. In the wake of the incident, the tanker's owner, Exxon, dispatched a ragtag crew with insufficient equipment, and it took six days for the shore cleanup to get underway. By then it was already a disaster, with a quarter of a million birds, more than 2,000 sea otters and 250 bald eagles dead. What's more, the local economy, which was based on fishing, was in ruins. Said one resident, "I don't think we are going to survive this one." A suit by locals against Exxon is still under appeal. The overall price tag to date for the oil giant runs to the billions. Public outcry led Congress to pass stringent regulations on tankers. Prince William Sound may never be the same, as oil from the sea floor continues to be stirred up by the tides and washed up on some beaches.

Scientists performing an autopsy on a gray whale that was beached on Kodiak Island in Alaska subsequent to the *Exxon Valdez* spill, 1989

Natalie Fobes/Corbis

Berlin Wall Crumbles

1989

As the German surrender on May 7, 1945, finally drew down the curtain on the European theater in World War II, it was time for the Allies to begin their occupation. The plan had been finalized earlier: There would be four zones, governed by the U.S.S.R., Great Britain, France and the U.S. The Soviets had the eastern sector—what would become East Germany. Berlin itself was similarly divided. By 1961, more than two million East Germans had fled to the West to escape totalitarian rule, and the loss of intellectuals and skilled workers was threatening the vitality of East Germany. The Soviet masters finally responded on August 13 by erecting a barbed wire fence that would later become a concrete barrier. Admission to the West was forbidden. Over the years nearly 200 would perish in the pursuit of freedom. The Wall became the chill, hard manifestation of the long cold war. In June 1987, with Soviet-American antagonism finally in a thaw, President Ronald Reagan called out in Berlin, "Mr. Gorbachev, tear down this wall!" The Soviet premier at last relented and, on November 9, 1989, the border was opened. West and East Germans scaled the Wall and met in full-throated celebration. "Wall woodpeckers" wielded hammers and chisels to gouge out souvenirs, and whole slabs were knocked down. As fireworks flared and car horns blared, Germany was united, and the Soviet Union was on the ropes.

An excited crowd dismantling the Berlin Wall, November 1989

Patrick Piel/Gamma

"Only connect!" urged E.M. Forster in his 1910 novel, *Howards End*. Seventy years later, Tim Berners-Lee, a British software consultant working at CERN, a particle physics laboratory near the Swiss Alps, heeded the call by writing a program that organized the fragmentary information swirling around in the Internet, a giant electronic post office without a consumer-friendly interface. The 1980 version, called Enquire Within Upon Everything, after a Victorian-era encyclopedia, allowed users to search and link files on their own computers. In 1990, Berners-Lee developed the World Wide Web, which enabled people to connect to one another's machines, sharing a seemingly infinite amount of information. "The dream behind the Web is of a common information space," he explained. "There was a second part of the dream, too, dependent on the Web being so generally used that it became a realistic mirror (or, in fact, the primary embodiment) of the ways in which we work and play and socialize." Today, hundreds of millions of people use it to chat with friends, conduct business, find cheap shoes or "enquire" about virtually everything. Not since Gutenberg's printing press 500 years earlier had the sharing of knowledge been so dramatically transfigured.

A young Berners-Lee soldering one of his first computers, 1976

1990

The World Wide Web

19 4
The End of Apartheid

"Cry, the beloved country, for the unborn child that is the inheritor of our fear. Let him not love the earth too deeply . . . For fear will rob him of all if he gives too much," wrote South African novelist Alan Paton in 1948. He was mourning the state of his country under the savage policy of apartheid. Black people were unable to move freely outside of their designated "homelands," which consisted of crowded shantytowns strangled by poverty and police intimidation. Resistance was met with brutality. Nelson Mandela, a charismatic leader in the fight to end apartheid, was sentenced to life in prison in 1964. Nearly 600 unarmed protesters were slain during a 1976 demonstration in Soweto; Steven Biko, their leader, was beaten by the police and died in their custody. Horrified governments around the world launched a boycott in the 1980s that crippled the South African economy. Shortly after his election in 1990, President F.W. de Klerk, under increasing pressure, began dismantling the repressive laws and freed Mandela, who won an easy victory in the 1994 election—the first in which blacks were permitted to vote. The country is still scarred by decades of inequality, but, as President Mandela declared: "The time for the healing of the wounds has come."

Mandela in Johannesburg, April 26, 1994, two days before the presidential election.

Brian Ferry, Remi Benali, Steve Walkowiak

1997

Dolly

People have been keeping sheep for at least 7,000 years, and there are today a billion of them on the planet. But throughout history, sheep have kept a very low profile . . . with one exception: Dolly was born on July 5, 1996, but her identity was unknown to the world at large until February 23, 1997, when Ian Wilmut, an embryologist at the Roslin Institute in Scotland, announced that he and a team of researchers had cloned her out of DNA taken from the udder of a six-year-old sheep. Clones, or genetic duplicates, had been made from embryos before that, but many scientists doubted it was possible to have adult DNA imitate DNA created by the meeting of sperm and egg. Dolly's name derived from the fact that her formative cell had come from a mammary gland, which suggested to the merry researchers the buxom performer Dolly Parton. Dolly the sheep seemed in every way normal, and gave birth to young of her own. Then, in March 2003, she developed a lung infection and had to be put down. She was six years old, and sheep can live to the age of 12. It is not certain whether the cloning played a part in her relatively short life. The advent of Dolly was, of course, a total stunner, as scientists and laymen alike wondered, loudly, how soon before the first cloned human, and what powers will lie in the hands of the one doing the cloning? A new door to medical advances had been opened, but so had a door to the unknown.

Ian Wilmut and Dolly, Midlothian, Scotland, M____ ___97

September 11

2001

The term *terrorism* was first used in the 1790s to describe the effects of mass execution and the guillotine during the French Revolution. At that time it was the state employing the tactics against the people, while terrorism today usually refers to violence directed against a regime. In recent decades, there have been dozens of examples of terrorism around the globe: Vietnam, Somalia, Northern Ireland, Italy et al. But through it all, the United States, within its borders, remained essentially free of the nightmare. There were random acts, certainly, but nothing that altered the American psyche. As dawn broke on September 11, 2001, it was just another Tuesday morning, and people went through the usual routine of getting ready for school or work, as they did any other day. That normalcy, that inherent peace of mind, was shattered for good shortly before nine a.m., Eastern Time, when American Airlines Flight 11 crashed into Tower No. 1 of New York City's World Trade Center. Minutes later a second jet crashed into the other Twin Tower and it was clear that there had been no accident. TV cameras were on the scene, and the nation and world were aghast—only to learn that at 9:41 a jetliner had blasted into the Pentagon. Then still another plane went down, this one in a Pennsylvania field. What would be next? was the jittery question, and it would be nightfall before the rumors and false reports drifted away. It was Day One in America's war against terrorism, and although the nation has lifted itself back up, the complex battle is now a part of our every day.

The morning of September 11, 2001, looking south past the Empire State Building to the World Trade Center, in New York City

Eric Feferberg/AFP/Getty

20○3 War in Iraq

Beginning in December 1998, Iraqi President Saddam Hussein refused to allow United Nations weapons inspections, fueling suspicion that he was stockpiling "weapons of mass destruction." President George W. Bush was convinced that WMDs were there,

Tsunami Sweeps Asia

For millions of years, two tectonic plates were slowly grinding together miles beneath the surface of the Indian Ocean, all the while building pressure. At 7:58 a.m. on December 26, 2004, six miles down, one plate snapped upward, causing a massive earthquake that sent shocks through the water, forming a powerful and deadly wave. This tsunami then blasted the coasts of South Asia and eastern Africa. A fisherman from Sumatra described being caught in his boat: "I heard this strange thunderous sound from somewhere, a sound I'd never heard before. I thought it was the sound of bombs. It felt like doomsday." The full extent of the tsunami's destruction will never be known, but estimates of lives lost surpass 250,000, with more than 100,000 still missing. Within hours, images of the destruction and ensuing suffering flooded cyberspace from camera phones and wi-fi laptops. In an inspired show of compassion, governments across the globe pledged $2 billion in aid in the week following the tragedy, and that total continued to rise. Private groups donated yet millions more. The U.N.'s emergency relief coordinator, Jan Egeland, said he had "never, ever seen such an outpouring of international assistance in any international disaster, ever."

The tsunami making shore in Koh Raya, near Phuket, Thailand, December 26, 2004

John Russell/The Age/Zuma

After conquering Relativity, the two-wheeler was a breeze for Einstein, here in 1933.